TOUGH QUESTIONS
CHRISTIANS ASK

TOUGH QUESTIONS CHRISTIANS ASK

EDITED BY DAVID NEFF

VICTOR BOOKS®
A DIVISION OF SCRIPTURE PRESS PUBLICATIONS INC.
USA CANADA ENGLAND

Recommended Dewey Decimal Classification: 230
Suggested Subject Heading: CHRISTIAN DOCTRINE & SPIRITUAL LIFE

Library of Congress Catalog Card Number: 88-62848
ISBN: 0-89693-623-6

Cover Illustration: Tim Jonke

CONTENTS

Understanding Christian Questions

David Neff

When I was a campus minister, I was frequently asked by students, "How can we know God exists?" At first I would shift into my apologetics mode, pull my philosophy of religion class notes from a mental filing cabinet, and repeat the classical arguments for God's existence.

But somewhere along the line, a student set me straight. She told me that the classic proofs were not at all what she was interested in. What she was really wondering about was how she could believe there was a God who cared for her, individually and personally, in light of the fact that she had not been accepted into medical school.

Ever after, when a student asked me how I knew God existed, I had a different reply: "Theologians and philosophers have debated that question for centuries, and they have come up with many good arguments for God's existence. I could tell you some of them, or give you a good book to read. But first, I am curious as to why you are asking the question. Has anything happened recently that has made this question important to you?"

Only once thereafter did I find a student who really wanted to know how to make the intellectual case for the existence of God.

This experience points up an important truth—namely, that we express our concerns for truth largely in relation to our experience. This is not to say that all truth questions are merely camouflage for what eats us relationally. It is rather to recognize that some questions about religious truth become compelling for certain people depending on their recent experience.

Similarly, the theological and theoretical questions we ask today may mask other questions. Questions about women in ministry or about the "good pagans" who follow other world religions can be just as much a vehicle for expressing unspoken feelings about sexual or cultural superiority. And, it has been pointed out, we ask about the trustworthiness of the Bible not only because some people raise actual objections to the veracity of Scripture, but because, as heirs of the Reformation, we need a nonecclesial court of appeal while resisting post-Enlightenment optimism toward human reason. Thus, as you find certain questions in this book striking a chord of recognition, ask yourself *why*.

Ultimately, all religious questions may be thought of as questions about God. "What will heaven be like?" is at bottom the question "What does the kind of heaven that Scripture hints at tell us about the God who rules there?" And the question "Does God have a plan for my life?" often boils down to the question "How much freedom does God grant me, and how good-hearted is he toward my falterings?"

Likewise, those who ask whether God will condemn to hell those who have never heard the name of Jesus may be less concerned about the eternal destiny of certain benighted Bantus and Watusis than they are about the fairness of God, and by implication, their own degree of comfort in his hands.

How this book came to be
Truth does not change. But the questions we ask about truth do. People in different stages of development or who occupy different stations in life find different questions compelling. And, thanks to broad cultural and philosophical movements, each age finds certain questions more pertinent than others.

In the high Middle Ages, scholars debated how many angels could dance on the head of a pin (really a question about the nature of ultimate reality), while monks and church officials disagreed over whether Christ had owned any property (a question about the legitimacy of the church's wealth).

What questions seem pertinent today? Wanting to tap the pulse of CHRISTIANITY TODAY readers, we mailed a survey to 475 randomly selected subscribers. We asked them to rate their interest in a series of common questions about Christian faith and practice. This was not a scientifically selected set of questions. (Indeed, the selection may tell you much about the editors of CHRISTIANITY TODAY.) Nevertheless we believe the results are instructive.

Readers were asked to rank their interest in the following questions on a scale of 1 to 5, with 1 representing "low interest" and 5 representing "high interest":

- Is the Bible completely accurate and trustworthy?
- Are creation and evolution incompatible?
- Is hell an ever-burning, physical place of torment? And is the Devil a personal being?
- Will a just God really condemn to hell people who have never heard of Jesus? Is Christianity the only religion through which people can know God?
- What will heaven be like? Will I know my loved ones in heaven?
- How can I be certain I will go to heaven? Will I be judged at the Last Judgment?
- Does Scripture give us a detailed look at the end times?
- Does God have a plan for my life, and if so, am I living it?
- How can a good God allow people to suffer?
- Is prosperity God's will for his people?
- Are biblical miracles intended for today?
- Does God continue to give messages to people today? Are there contemporary prophets who speak for God?
- Do I need to be an active member of a church to live a Christian life?
- Should women hold ordained leadership positions in churches?
- Should Christians take their Sabbath/Sunday observances more seriously?
- Is the charismatic renewal, seen in many churches today, from God?
- How involved should Christians be in the political process?

When we tallied the results, the question about Sabbath/Sunday observance had the highest number of "high interest" ratings of any question on the list. Sixty-four percent of the readers who returned the survey gave this question a 4 or a 5. Other questions with ratings close behind were "Does God have a plan for my life?" (62 percent); "Does God continue to give messages to people today?" (61 percent); and "Should women hold ordained leadership positions in churches?" (60 percent).

The proximity of these top ratings and the size of the sample suggest that we exercise caution in making too much of the results. Yet, because we were not expecting the Sabbath/Sunday question to come anywhere near the top of the list—much less right at the top— we believe the results show that conservative Christians take the issue of the Lord's Day very seriously. And thus we begin this book with Eugene Peterson's intensely personal essay on this subject.

But you need not feel obligated to begin with that chapter. Look at the Table of Contents and see what interests you. Then read those chapters first, asking yourself why these issues seem important to you. Eventually, you will want to read all the chapters, because by exposing ourselves to the questions that stretch other people, we grow in our understanding not only of truth but of our fellow Christians.

If you find that a question important to you is missing from this book, and I am sure you will, please drop a letter or postcard to my attention at CHRISTIANITY TODAY. (The address is 465 Gundersen Drive, Carol Stream, IL 60188.) The editors will give your suggestions due attention (although we will not have time to respond personally to every letter), and we may include your concern in a forthcoming book or magazine article.

Many authors make light work. As do typists, proofreaders, typesetters, and copy editors. Special thanks is due Elizabeth Gretz, now employed at Harvard University Press, who copy edited most of this book's chapters; Marty White, CHRISTIANITY TODAY's editorial coordinator, who kept the work flowing; and the Senior Editors, the quintet of scholars who advise the editors of CHRISTIANITY TODAY, and who made excellent suggestions for the selection of the authors of these chapters. Any errors in judgment or accuracy are entirely my responsibility.

Chapter 1

SHOULD CHRISTIANS PAY CLOSER ATTENTION TO THE LORD'S DAY?

Eugene H. Peterson

Sabbath keeping has a bad name among American Christians. Yet when CHRISTIANITY TODAY *asked its readers to rate the importance of various religious questions, the Lord's Day question was most frequently marked "important" or "very important." Was it just the product of residual guilt feelings absorbed from our Puritan past? Or is there a deeper need that Sabbaths can fill?*

Here Pastor Eugene Peterson, author of Reversed Thunder: The Revelation of John and the Praying Imagination, *shares his own experience and his hopes for American believers.*

I caught on to it early, and engaged in my sin with gusto. As I developed in the Christian faith, I was examined and instructed in ways to discern, repent of, and defend against the classic sins that interfered with faith and love and hope.

When I became a pastor, I was subject to even more rigorous examination. Not once did anyone call me on this sin. Instead, I was—if you can believe it—commended in my law breaking. At one critical point in my life, when I was obsessively out of control in my indulgence of this sin, I was rewarded with the largest single annual increase in salary I have ever received.

It is the only sin I know of that a Christian can commit not only with impunity but with applause. Not bad. It has all the exhilaration of breaking the rules, with none of the consequences—at least none of the social consequences. With such built-in blessings and such a handsome payback, it is little wonder that this tops the charts as the favorite sin among Christians. It is the one sin we can indulge to our heart's content—and get praised as saints in the very act.

It is the American bargain-basement sin, on sale in virtually every American church, with a free instruction manual thrown in. The sin? Sabbath breaking, the willful violation of the fourth commandment.

I saw this sin rampant in others long before I saw it in myself. What I saw was not attractive: an entire culture living on the edge of panic. A mind-boggling technology that could do almost anything in and with space, but fidgety, nervous, and spastic with time. I saw the people around me work masterfully with computers, organizations, and electronic equipment, but when presented with an unplanned or undefined ten minutes, hour, or day, they were suddenly overtaken with the Saint Vitus' Dance. They could not stand still. They could not be still. And I began to observe the results.

• Ugliness proliferating: If travelers no longer look long and lovingly at the landscape, why bother with beauty? Stick up a billboard.

• Divorce rampant: If spouses no longer look long and lovingly at each other, why bother with faithfulness? A "meaningful relationship" is a lot easier.

• Families angry and violent: If parents and children no longer look long and lovingly at one another, why bother to listen? Get your way by yelling and hitting.

• Addictions epidemic: If men and women no longer look long and lovingly at limitations, why bother with discipline? Transcend with a drink or a needle.

• Religion merchandised: If Christians no longer look long and lovingly at God, why bother with the mysteries of faith, the unpredictabilities of amazing grace? Buy a plain and easy answer. Buy some sure-fire good feelings.

The common thread running through all this is the refusal to be still and be silent. It is the refusal to look and listen; the refusal that then becomes an inability to stop and rest and behold what is "very good" in the Creation and in the Cross. Is God doing anything in this world? Is God saying anything to this people?

Who knows? If anyone is going to find out, it will require some first-class ("long and loving") looking and listening, the kind of first-class looking and listening that Sabbath-keeping nurtures and matures.

Sloth

The source sin of Sabbath breaking is sloth. But isn't sloth doing nothing at all? No, sloth is doing nothing of what we were created to do as beings made in the image of God and saved by the Cross of Christ. Sloth is laziness at the center, while the periphery is adazzle with a torrent of activity and talk. Laziness, the seventh of the deadly sins, is the lazy refusal to do our real work—deal with God, deal with ourselves. It is the sin that unobtrusively avoids Creator-attentiveness and creature-awareness, and then noisily and busily diverts attention from the great avoidance with a smoke screen of activity.

The stereotype of a sloth—that three-toed creature hanging indolent and useless from its branch in the rain forest—is a far cry from what we actually do. The sin of sloth nimbly dodges the fundamental human task of being attentive to God, of being self-aware as a creature of God. This attentiveness and awareness is hard and quiet work. We would rather do almost anything else, but we would also like not to be caught out in our laziness. So we talk fast and move fast. We impress people with our activity and responsibilities and full schedules. People admire us for getting so much done and for being so involved in the world, and they flatter us by saying that they could not get along without us. Overactivity, overwork, overinvolvement are, each one, a cover for sloth. Sloth utilizes the technique of the Big Lie.

Christians are in the vanguard of this sin, and they escape detection even more successfully than the non-Christian because they label this sloth-derived hyperactivity with euphemisms: "ministry," "witness," "the Lord's work." They pretend to keep a Sabbath by Sunday churchgoing, and then stuff the day with meetings, responsibilities, committees, and concerns until it looks (and feels) as tight as a German sausage. Pastors are usually in charge of the stuffing.

I looked at this sloth-activated Sabbath breaking and was staggered by its ruinous effects in the culture, in the church, and in myself. The social evil and personal misery resulting from Sabbath desecration far exceed that of adultery and murder combined. The incredible shoddiness in personal relationships that characterizes our culture is more than anything else a consequence of sins against time—for intimacy requires time, affection requires time. Without time neither the best of intentions nor the highest standard of living penetrates the human relationships through which we realize our dignity and our worth. And the outrageous adolescence in religion that is the scandal of our churches is, more than anything else, a consequence of sins against time—for maturity requires time, worship requires time. Without time—rhythmic, unhurried, expectant time—neither the most sincere conversion nor the most ardent commitment penetrates our lives and becomes sane, mature, and wise holiness.

Doing anything about the sloth in American culture seemed beyond me, and in church culture even more so. But I thought I might do something about myself.

A personal Sabbath

I started by keeping a Sabbath myself. Sunday is a workday for me, and it is therefore unavailable as a Sabbath. I decided to keep a Monday Sabbath. My wife joined me in the observance. We agreed that it would be a true Sabbath, and not a "day off." We didn't have much to follow in the way of precedents, since few of the Christians and none of the pastors of our acquaintance kept a Sabbath, but we knew that it must be a day for praying and playing, the two elements we noticed were woven in and out of the healthy biblical, Jewish, and Christian observances.

We knew we needed a place and a routine (a sanctuary and a ritual) to support our practice. We chose to use the forest trails for our sanctuary and devised a simple ritual of silence for the morning hours; we break the silence over lunch with audible prayers and are free to converse through the afternoon and evening. We watch birds, smell flowers, pray the psalms, feel the weather, reflect, listen, look. Intending to be as diligent in our Sabbath keeping as we want our parishioners to be in theirs, we keep these Monday Sabbaths in all kinds of weather and whether we feel like it or not. No other single thing that we have ever done comes close to being as creative and deepening in our marriage, our ministry, and our faith.

A congregational Sabbath

I began to want this for my congregation, too. I saw them mostly as victims of a culture that had been subverted by "angel of light" tactics without anyone even noticing, for they genuinely supposed their Sabbath breaking to be virtuous and were accustomed to pastoral commendation for their sloth. I wanted to recover, if possible, the vast leisure of contemplation, recover the Sabbath margins to the week that would allow for joy and dignity. I was not in a position to impose a common observance; I did not want even to hint at a guilt-trap legalism. I knew how long it had taken me to recognize the actual virulence in the apparently virtuous charades of my own sloth, and how difficult it is to stand against the pressures of the culture. I determined to provide them with worship that was centered, surrounded, and rooted in prayer—not a day for recruitment, entertainment, or launching projects. I tried to keep Sundays free for them, free from church business and free for worship; free from my work and free for their leisure. I knew this was going to take a long time and that it could only be realized incrementally.

After several years of this behind-the-scenes "not doing," I came out in the open with a letter to the congregation: "Why Your Pastor Wants You to Keep a Sabbath."

> One day a week I stand before you and call you to worship God. The conviction behind the act is that time is holy. But how often do you hear anyone say so? More likely you hear

that "time is money." And as with money, you mostly feel that you don't have enough of it, ever. On occasion, when you have time for which nothing is scheduled, you will "kill time."

Odd, isn't it? We have more leisure hours per person per year as a country than anyone could have guessed a hundred years ago. But we are not leisurely. We are not relaxed. We are anxious. We are in a hurry. The anxiety and the hurry ruin intimacy and sabotage our best intentions in faith, hope, and love—the three actions in which most of us set out to do our best.

That is why I as your pastor want you to keep a Sabbath. I want you to live well. I want you to live whole and mature, with appreciation and pleasure, experiencing the heights and depths of God's glory in your bodies and your work, your friends and your gardens, your minds and your emotions, at the ocean and in the mountains. You can't do that if you are "on the run." You can't do that if you are watching the clock.

Sabbath is the biblical tool for protecting time against desecration. It is the rhythmic setting apart of one day each week for praying and playing—the two activities for which we don't get paid, but which are necessary for a blessed life. A blessed life is what we are biblically promised. A blessed life is not a mere survival life but a bountiful life. Praying and playing are warp and woof in the bounty.

"Sabbath" is the Hebrew word for "stop"—a stop sign on the street of days. Stop what you are doing and look around, see what is going on. And listen. What is going on? God, mostly. God creating; God saving; God providing; God blessing; God speaking. God does us the great honor of inviting us in as co-workers in his Genesis work. We participate in the creating, saving, providing, blessing, speaking. It is good work. When we do it well we are exhilarated. When we do it badly we are bored. The world of work, a powerful field of energy, demands a great deal of us. But in the midst of the work we can easily lose touch with the origin of our work and its purpose, the peace of our work and its rhythms. Instead of feeling the creativity of work, we become compulsive. Instead of feeling the freedom and dignity of work, we feel trapped and demeaned. And so at the end of each work week God calls a Sabbath. We stop. Our work—our lives—open into freedom, into leisured goodness, into God-ness.

Keeping a Sabbath is simple and easy: we pray and we play, two things we were pretty good at as children, and can always pick up again with a little encouragement if we can only find the time. But we don't have to find the time, it is given to us. A day a week. A Sabbath. A day to pray and play. God's gift.

Christian practice orients the first element of the day around the act of worship—praying. This is the great act of freedom in relation to Heaven. This is the exercise of our bodies and minds in acts of adoration and commitment, supplication and praise, ventures of forgiving and giving. We explore, enjoy, and share it in our assembly for worship. For most of you this praying will start out in our sanctuary each Sunday when I call you to worship God. Simple.

The second element of the day is for playing. This is the great act of freedom in relation to Earth. We exercise our bodies and minds in games and walks, in amusement and reading, in visiting and picnicking, in puttering and writing. We take in the colors and shapes, the sounds and smells. We let the creativity of the creation nudge us into creativity. We surprise ourselves by creating a meal, or a conversation, or an appreciation, or some laughter that wasn't in our job description. We have some fun. Easy.

So—if it is so simple and easy, why do we find it so hard? Because the world is in a conspiracy to steal our Sabbath. It is a pickpocket kind of theft (nothing like an armed robbery) and we aren't aware of it until long after its occurrence. The "world" is sometimes our friends, sometimes our families, sometimes our employers—they want us to work for them, not waste time with God, not be our original selves. If the world can get rid of our Sabbath, it has us to itself. What it does with us when it gets us is not very attractive: after a few years of Sabbath breaking we are passive consumers of expensive trash and anxious hurriers after fantasy pleasures. We lose our God and our dignity at about the same time.

That is why I want you to keep a Sabbath. Guard the day. Protect the leisure for praying and playing. There are no rules for this: the furthest thing from my intent is to oppress you with restrictions. My pastoral purpose is to recover the gift of the day, this marvelous day that protects our inner (praying) and outer (playing) selves from desecrations of greed and pride, this day that every seven days reintroduces us to a Creation-freedom, a Christ-freedom. Unlike Christians in earlier generations, we get no help from our culture in keeping the Sabbath. But it does not seem to me wise to compensate by setting up regulations or procedures. I leave you free to work out the specifics on your own. What we must do is focus our intent, and then help each other by praying together each Sunday in the name of Jesus who taught us to pray, and playing in honor of Christ—"for Christ plays in ten thousand places / Lovely in limbs, and lovely in eyes not his / To the Father through the features of men's faces" (G. M. Hopkins).

Sabbath islands

I didn't expect a rush of compliance in response to the letter; nor was I disappointed. But here and there, now and then, individuals, and sometimes families, venture into the practice of Sabbath keeping, and work out ways to participate in the sanctification of time in the particular circumstances of their own temperaments, routines, jobs, and schedules.

Sabbath keeping, at least in our American culture, cannot (must not!) be imposed. It can only be realized by the person of faith who—following the counsel of Jesus, who told us that we were not made for the Sabbath, but the Sabbath for us (Mark 2:27)—is caught by a sense of reverence and grace inherent in time and wills to honor it in rhythmic faithfulness through a lifetime of weeks. I have in my imagination a picture of coral formations in an ocean, gradually but surely growing, eventually accreting into an island that emerges out of the watery chaos, a safe place for the shipwrecked to land. These Sabbath islands appear from time to time, from place to place, the consequence of praying-playing Christians who mock the noisy pretensions of the world's winds and waves by attending to God, and to themselves before God. Each Sabbath act is a grain that adheres to another, Sabbath to Sabbath, and unlikely as it seems, through a process of organic accretion lifts a time-island above the fretful seas. These islands in ages past became continents, and could become so again.

High-risk territory

But I must post a warning here: This Sabbath keeping is incredibly perilous. The casualties to worship and discipleship are statistically staggering. Keeping the Lord's Day holy is as dangerous to soul and spirit as driving an automobile at high speeds is to life and limb. The holy-day carnage in homes and churches rivals, and probably exceeds, the holiday death count on our highways. For every Christian who experiences this day as redolent with freedom and sunny with grace, there seem to be a dozen who tell stories of childhood Sundays corseted with whalebone prohibitions. This surely is a terrible irony, that the day that has been enjoyed and celebrated by so many as Queen Sabbath should enter the lives of children and converts as an ugly witch. It is too little noticed and remarked upon that among the numerous and solemn commands in Scripture to keep the Sabbath are some extraordinarily fierce condemnations of those who kept it in such a way that was ruinous to them and to everyone around them.

Isaiah, with angry sarcasm, calls Sabbath keeping the "trampling" of God's courts: "new moon and Sabbath and the calling of assemblies—I cannot endure iniquity and solemn assembly. . . . They have become a burden to me" (Isa. 1:13–14). Hosea (2:11), Amos (8:5), and Jeremiah (ch. 7) are equally strident in their denunciations of Sabbath keepers. Jesus received more hostile criticism from Sabbath keepers than from any other single class of people. Paul was irritably impatient with people who were insistent on a recovery of Sabbath keeping (see Rom. 14:5–9; Gal. 4:8–10).

Every Christian who agrees to keep a Sabbath enters high-risk territory. But if Sabbath keeping is so prone to abuse, so liable to hypocritical pretension, is it wise to ask for compliance? It is wise, but the counsel must not be given naïvely—this is a dangerous practice. But it is no more dangerous than the practice of marriage, the rearing of children, or the worship of God. Whenever we are working at the optimum of our powers as human beings, the temptations to evil are also at their height. *Corruptio optimi pessima* (When the best is corrupted, it becomes the worst).

The surest way to keep Sabbath keeping honest and holy is to return the practice continuously to its biblical reasons. In its basic form the Sabbath command is given twice, first in Exodus, then in Deuteronomy, but each time with a different reason. The Exodus explanation is that God rested on the seventh day, marking it with blessing and holiness. Sabbath keeping gets us into step with the rhythm of the Creator. It is a day for praying (Exod. 20:8–11). The

Deuteronomy reason is that the people had been saved from Egyptian slavery, which had lasted 400 years without a day off. Sabbath keeping gets us into step with the rhythm of the Savior. It is social justice, the gracious relief from the oppression of sin. It is a day for playing (Deut. 5:12–15).

How we keep the day is not biblically prescribed. That we keep the day is commanded. By giving us clear reasons that lay the foundation for Sabbath keeping, and by not giving instructions on how to implement them in our situation, has not our Lord the Spirit dignified us with creativity and initiative? He trusts us to work out practices of prayer and play that honor and participate in holiness. Should we not be equally trusting of each other and diligently refrain from imposing methods of Sabbath keeping? There is scope for endless creativity here when we encourage a return to the source reasons of praying and playing.

Praying and playing
Praying is the action by which we attend to God, stretching out in daring acts of intimacy beyond ourselves, risking ourselves in meetings on holy ground, where there is no guarantee that we will come back alive. Praying is the instinctive act of responding to our Creator, of pleading to our Savior, of praising our Provider. Everyone does it: children and adults, the primitive tribes and civilized nations, paleolithic hunters and space-age astronauts. From time to time people quit doing it. Gradually life flattens into two-dimensional predictability.

Playing is the action by which we explore our humanity, experiment with the movements of our body, discover and test limits, enter into the swift and kaleidoscopic energies of other persons in combinations of opposition and cooperation, heighten the interplay of space and time in their multiple diversities: velocity and shape, color and interval, pattern and rhythm, mass and silence. Playing extends the range of human experience, and in the process we find that we like being human—play exhilarates, gives pleasure. Everyone does it. But not all the time. Some people withdraw from the game entirely. When they do, the people around them feel diminished, feel that there is less humanity in the room, in the town.

Integration

Both playing and praying are essential for good Sabbath keeping. A Sabbath that omits one or the other is not a true Sabbath. But it is difficult to integrate them. Our commonest experience is with their separation. In America we have conspicuous examples of widespread observance of half-Sabbaths: prayerful Sabbaths without any play, and playful Sabbaths without any prayer. Our Puritan ancestors practiced the first; our pagan contemporaries practice the second.

The Puritan America of 200 years ago was good at Lord's Day prayer but gave play short shrift. The Puritans were on a serious expedition, intent as they were on establishing the "city on the hill." Prayer and work were the yoked oxen of their enterprise. Prayer came to have less and less to do with adoring God and became more and more utilitarian—a supernatural assist to making a profit. Tragically, and unbiblically, they left out, and in some instances actually banned, play. Though this did wonders for the economy, it blighted the human spirit into a dutiful but cheerless religion.

The pagan America of today is good at Lord's Day play, but is anemic in prayer. The revival of pagan enthusiasm for the body fills sports stadiums and crowds recreation areas with persons on a religious quest for fun. The occasional prayers offered are on the model of ritual incantations supplicating the Greek Fates for a favorable breeze. By trivializing prayer, their lives are trivialized and the play that they had expected to give them pleasure leaves them greedy, anxious, and fatigued. Such play, instead of venturing into an exploratory celebration of being human, becomes an escape from the human and dehumanizes the players.

The Christian task is to combine them, to integrate and mature them—this Sabbath praying and Sabbath playing—in glorious gospel Sabbath keeping. Every day that is kept holy in these biblical ways is leaven in the week, salt in the year. Christians serious about the redemption of a Devil-harassed society and about sharing our Lord's invitation to "all who labor and are heavy laden" (Matt. 11:28) can hardly make a better beginning than by enacting with their lives Sabbaths that carve out time for long and loving looks at Christ and his creatures. This cannot be accomplished by a Panzer assault: bully preaching or blue laws. But as a few Christians in a few churches in a few communities in America keep a Sabbath, pockets of resistance are formed that provide access to leisured and loving time for the people around them, in the same way that national parks preserve access to the beauties of wilderness space. These pockets of hidden holiness preserve our days and keep each week accessible to creation work and resurrection appearances.

Chapter 2

SHOULD CHRISTIANS BE INVOLVED IN POLITICS?

Rodney Clapp

"Politics as usual"—as that phrase gains meaning from the likes of Boss Tweed—gives many Christians a feeling of ritual defilement. But as dirty as governmental politics often is, there is another kind of politics we cannot avoid. The routine of daily living (how we organize family life, treat laborers, or transfer real estate, for example) is intensely political. And we cannot retreat from these basic questions (without taking strict vows of chastity and poverty, that is).

Here CHRISTIANITY TODAY senior writer Rodney Clapp, author with Robert Webber of People of the Truth: The Power of the Worshiping Community in the Modern World *(Harper & Row), explains the essentially political nature of biblical truth and shows how biblical politics and the business of government can best interact.*

Mabs Walker—grandmother, bank teller, Sunday school teacher—has a problem. She has attended the same Presbyterian church in the same medium-sized Pennsylvania town all her life. In fact, it is a church in which her father was treasurer for 25 years; her grandfather and grandmother were founding members. The funerals for her parents and grandparents were conducted there. She was baptized and married there, and so were both of her daughters. When she enters the church each Sunday, it is as if the pews and stained-glass windows dance with memories. This is where many of the most important events of her life have occurred, and she cannot really identify who she is without referring to First Presbyterian.

Her problem is that a new young preacher has come to the church. Mabs is a big-hearted and lively person, and she recognizes the need to let new pastors make some changes. But this pastor is saying there is no gospel without political action. He preaches constantly about Nicaragua and the threat of nuclear war. His Sunday evening series has focused for the last eleven weeks on a Christian approach to sexism. And last week he asked Mabs to distribute to the children in her Sunday school class white balloons bearing the words "Christ died for everyone, even the Russians."

First Presbyterian, in short, is becoming a very different church. Mabs cares about the plight of people in El Salvador and Afghanistan, but it is hard for her to relate all these issues to her daily concerns. "My life has nothing to do with politics," she says. She is worried about the young couple who attended a few weeks ago, curious about what Presbyterian Christians believe, and who heard only that the treatment of the homeless in this country is a national shame. And when a friend of hers whose husband died recently went to the pastor for counseling, she was simply referred to a local psychotherapist. Mabs is more patient than many of her fellow parishioners, but even she muttered last week, "The church was so much better before it had anything to do with politics."

"First Presbyterian" is a gross exaggeration, of course. Few, if any, actual churches are quite so politically saturated. But many churches are much more "political" than they used to be, and not all are leaning to the Left. Many list to the Right. There is a loud chorus of voices insisting that Christians must be politically involved. They must save America, or they must save the world from America. And most of us, like Mabs, feel confused. Jesus clearly calls us to be concerned for the poor, the helpless children, and the widowed. We see and wholeheartedly affirm the good of the civil rights movement, born in and sustained by the church. The number of abortions performed each year in our nation is extremely disturbing, and the family, so much a part of our life in the church, does seem threatened by some powerful trends in our society. So we can agree that the church should be politically involved. But how? And how much?

Of course, there is no neat computation through which we can determine in some sure and accurate way what is appropriate political involvement. But maybe we can make a little more sense of the problem by taking a closer look at Mabs and her church. At first, however, things will seem even more confusing, because our initial conclusion is not that either Mabs or the new preacher is right, but that both are wrong.

Depth politics

Mabs is wrong because she thinks her life has "nothing to do with politics." It is true that she does not go to town meetings or write letters to her senator. But that kind of politics concerns only governmental issues. There is another kind.

Philosophers tell us that every society must deal with five essential matters: parent-child relationships; truth telling; the sanctity of life; how people hold and what they do with belongings; and the sexual ordering of society.

Not all societies agree on how to handle these matters. Some, for example, honor their elderly by leaving them to freeze to death in the arctic wastes; others place their weakening parents in nursing homes. Some say property belongs to the state; others say it belongs to individuals. Some say the lives of people of all races should be protected; others say a white life is more valuable than a black life.

There are differences in how societies organize themselves around these five core issues, but all societies do organize themselves around them—in one way or another. They must. A society will not last long if it has no appreciation of honesty and leaves its members only to doubt and be afraid of what each person really wants. Its children will not live to adulthood (and thus to the point at which they can bear children and repopulate the society) if its parents have no concern to help their children thrive past infancy. And if there is not some sort of distribution of goods, people will starve and die in the rain, which will lead a society to revolution or to simple disintegration.

People will not survive, let alone prosper, without some ordering of their life together. This ordering of our life together is a *polis*, a gathering of persons characterized by a sense of community, and from *polis* we get our word *political*. So politics, in the broadest sense, underlies and permeates society.

Politics in this sense—what we might call "depth politics"—has always been a part of Mabs's church. She was married there, after all. It was her church, representing the Christian faith, that gave her and her husband the idea that they should publicly commit themselves to one another, instead of simply moving in together (and that gave Mabs's husband the idea that he should have one wife rather than five or six). It was some friends in the church, trying to live up to the Christian ideal of fidelity, who helped the Walkers avoid a divorce at a rough point in their marriage. Mabs's children were baptized at the church, suggesting to her that she must care for them in the love of Christ.

The unavoidable fact is that we do not live fully human, personal lives as solitary individuals. We are personal—we come to be persons—as individuals relating to other individuals. Personal life is life together, and all of our life together is based on a certain vision of what the good life should be. We shape and form our life together in an attempt to achieve that good life. There are many ways to envision and organize life together, of course. The Christian way of life offers a vision of life based on the way Christ lived and died, and it calls Christians to live together in a particular fashion—namely, in service to one another and to the world.

In the sense of depth politics, the Bible is profoundly and thoroughly political. All parts of the biblical story have, though they are not exhausted by, political dimensions. At Creation God makes man male and female, an incipient society, and leaves guidelines on how life together should proceed ("A man will leave his father and mother and be united to his wife," Gen. 2:24, NIV). He also makes man and woman the stewards, or organizers and caretakers, of the rest of creation. The Fall is, among other things, an attempt at political revolution, with God's sovereignty defied through the lure of a rebel to his rule. Redemption involves the calling out of a special people, a new polity to witness God's loving rule to the world—first Israel and then the new "holy nation" that is the church (1 Pet. 2:9). Finally, at the Consummation, the perfection of his redemption, God will call his beloved to live together in a city, the perfect *polis* (Rev. 21:2).

Reading the Bible, then, cannot help affecting our vision of the good life and how people should live together, and this has undeniably been the case. It is dangerous and misleading to speak of any "Christian nation," but the biblical story has done much to shape Western societies. Historians agree that the idea of one God for all peoples, whatever their race, class, or sex, fundamentally informs the democratic vision. Christians and nominal Christians were slaveholders in nascent America, but never entirely comfortably. (Thomas Jefferson, for instance, recognized that the words of his Declaration of Independence were contradicted by his own slave-holding.) Historians also commonly observe that Marxism derived the hope of a classless society—its heaven on Earth—from the biblical expectation of the coming kingdom. Thus, even Western atheism is different from what it might have been had our societies never been influenced by Christianity.

All this means that Mabs Walker is wrong to think that her life or her faith has nothing to do with politics. Depth politics is pervasive. But all this also means that her pastor is wrong. He thinks the church has nothing to do with politics unless it engages, more or less directly, in governmental politics. So now we see that it is somewhat misleading merely to ask: Should the church get politically involved? We do better to divide that question into two more promising queries: How should the church get involved in depth politics? And how should it get involved in governmental politics?

A transcendent loyalty
In a general way, the church's contributions to depth politics flow from its recognition that it serves a transcendent God. To the Christian, no government or political party is ultimate; all are liable

to the judgment of God. United under the lordship of Christ, the church should be a place in which persons with contradictory political programs can meet and listen with respect for one another. Possessing a common loyalty higher than their temporal political loyalty, Christians gather at the Lord's Table together. Figuratively speaking, some may not speak to others more than to ask for the salt to be passed, but that is still the beginning of communication. We cannot easily dismiss a brother or sister in Christ, and therefore the church is a place where political opponents are not dehumanized or demonized (at least ideally, which, given the tribalism so brazenly recurring in history, is no small gain).

The church's dedication to a transcendent loyalty also means it is not restricted to the "necessities" presented by political and social systems. Slavery was once considered a necessity. The Christian vision, able to see beyond perishable societies and economies, played a large part in gradually eliminating that "necessity." Nowadays many Americans act as if sexual impulses of any sort must necessarily be indulged, and teenagers are not encouraged to see sexual abstinence as a realistic option. Able to see beyond biological "necessity," Christians can contribute to a better sexual ethic for a confused society. There are other examples: whether believers in pacifism or in the just-war tradition, all Christians follow the Prince of Peace and so must stand constantly ready to challenge authorities who insist violence is necessary; and Christians will not be easily convinced that, in any given situation, poverty is necessary. The point is simply that, open to the transcendent, the church lives and can suffuse society with a healing and abundant creativity.

This does not mean the church is utopian. On the contrary, an appreciation of transcendence inculcates in Christians a gritty realism. Those who dream of the kingdom of God are keenly aware of human limitations and sin. For all the world's talk about *realpolitik*, about politics based on practical and material factors rather than on theoretical or ethical objectives, it is difficult for politicians to be realistic and truthful. In democracies, on the one hand, politicians must tell voters what they want to hear. Very few candidates, for instance, honestly admit they will raise taxes, and of those very few, even fewer win elections. (And not all the blame for dishonesty should fall on those who govern; those who are governed do not really want to hear the truth.) In authoritarian states, on the other hand, those who hold power routinely misrepresent reality to further their own cause. There is thus a need everywhere for a body of people who can be truthful, who can admit finitude and the tragic pervasiveness of sin. Such a body is the church.

Transcendence is the key to many of the church's most significant depth political contributions to society. This transcendence is not vaguely defined; we learn what it means through the revelation of God in Christ. Hearing and rehearsing the story of Jesus in worship forms a people who live according to the pattern of the Cross. Within the church, Christians refer constantly to this story and rightly speak in its terms.

But what about when they attempt to address the wider society, a world that knows little of Jesus' cross and certainly refuses to pick it up and bear it? Much, perhaps most, of the church's depth politics will not directly engage government. The church, simply by living according to its alternative polity, will challenge and encourage the surrounding society. Yet some issues will inevitably come to involve law and the administration of social programs. This fact moves us closer to governmental politics.

A second language
It is at this point, of course, that the church-and-politics debate really heats up. Some might think the church should simply involve itself with depth politics and stop at that. After all, stepping into partisan, governmental politics often means losing a perspective rooted in the transcendent, exactly the church's unique contribution to society's good.

Yet, as we have mentioned, governmental politics often impinge directly on the mission and life of the church. And the Bible evidences a clear concern for systemic as well as individual justice. Finally, it is especially true in a technological world, with central-ized economies (whether capitalist or state-controlled), that much human good and ill can come from the exercise of governmental politics. That given, can the church retain its crucial rootedness in the Christian transcendent and simultaneously speak to a world rejecting that transcendent?

It can. Initially the church must recognize that it speaks a unique "language," the language of a people who risk their lives on the story of Jesus Christ. This is a different language than that used by those outside the church, and the world cannot be wholly and truly understood, Christians believe, without using this language. It is a mistake to think there is some religious essence—Buddhist, Hindu, Shinto, Tao, or other—that can be translated into any language with equal verity.

But this means that Christians who want to affect governmental politics must learn a second language. They cannot expect non-Christians, in a pluralistic society, to use the unique Christian language for public discourse. When the church learns a second language, the language for public discourse, it can do two things.

First, it can hold government to its own highest ideals. This is, in part, what Christian abolitionists did in their struggle to end slavery in the United States. Their understanding of freedom was fundamentally based on their faith that Christ died for all people. Yet they did not need to refer (though many did) to uniquely Christian language when debating slavery. They needed only to point to the highest ideals of the nation, as stated in its own founding documents, and slavery was strikingly undercut. Every government claims to work for the good of its people; the church can fairly ask, "Are you working for the good of the people, *on your own terms?*"

Second, the church, having learned a second language, can subtly use insights from its own first language to redefine the terms of public debate. Consider the campaign slogan, "Are you better off than you were four years ago?" Christians might accept the question as valid, but then suggest to their neighbors that economics is not the only measurement of being "better off." The question might imply not only "Are you better off because you have a larger house?" but "Are you better off because your life has more meaning than it did?" Not only "Are you better off because inflation is less threatening?" but "Are you better off because you have a more tightly knit family, more friends, happier neighbors?" Gradually, then, the debate may be shifted from narrower to broader, more generous grounds, and it may even be rephrased from "Are *you* better off?" to "Are *we* better off?"

These levels of involvement—between depth and governmental politics—are open to all Christians. But there is also the even more intensive involvement of those Christians who work within government. These Christians are often criticized by their fellow believers because they must compromise to participate in government. A distinction is crucial: Christians (and others) who practice government do not compromise their beliefs; they compromise on certain applications of those beliefs. Admittedly, the relation between belief and application is sometimes agonizingly close, but it is important to remember that Christians can disagree on the application of truth, even a fundamental truth, without disagreeing on truth itself. In general, an openness to political compromise is an affirmation of biblical truth rather than a denial of it. To recognize compromise on these matters is to recognize that our endeavors, no matter how grand or well intended, are not absolute. They may point to the kingdom of God, but they never embody it.

A politically involved church
Though we may seem to have gone far from Mabs Walker and her small Pennsylvania church, a clearer understanding of depth and governmental politics is relevant to her situation. Imagine that Mabs and her minister, after a seminar on the church and politics, were able to agree on the fundamentals sketched above. Let us say that Mabs now recognizes that politics, in its broader and its narrower senses, has something to do with church. And let us say also that her pastor recognizes that politics, especially in its narrower, governmental sense, is not the only matter of concern to the church. Finally, let us say that they agree to attack the community and national problem of drugs.

Mabs and the pastor decide they must first help themselves and the rest of their church to understand drug usage with their unique "first" language; that is, they must learn to view the problem theologically, through the revelation of God in Christ.

In subsequent Sunday school classes, members of First Presbyterian realize that our society encourages the use of all kinds of drugs—legal as well as illegal—to eliminate an unending list of ills quickly and painlessly. They recognize that they should be thankful for drugs that eliminate polio and cure pneumonia. But they also reflect on the story told in Scripture: Sin breaks the world, and the world is saved only by the sacrificial death of its Savior. This story means that suffering cannot be entirely mended in this lifetime: no drug can cure loneliness or mend a broken heart. In other words, people remain limited and fallen, though with hope—but hope only in a transcendent, gracious God, not in themselves or their concoctions.

On the level of depth politics, then, First Presbyterian comes to recognize that the roots of the drug problem lie within all of us who have been conditioned to find quick, painless, technological fixes for our problems and to expect the same for even our most profound discontents. First Presbyterian realizes that its own children will not be able to "just say no" if societal example and insinuation continue to shout, "Yes, yes, yes!" It is driven to teach more intensively the truth of the Cross, that suffering is sometimes ineradicable but can be redemptive.

Moving out from its depth political concerns, First Presbyterian sponsors a seminar for the public. It presents several educational films, opens a forum for debate on the need for a drug-control center in town, and has the pastor speak—without explicit reference to the Bible—about the power of drugs in our society. The pastor challenges all listeners to recognize how much we depend on drugs such as alcohol, caffeine, and tranquilizers, and to see the relation between that "dependency" and the pressure for some, especially young people, to depend on much more harmful drugs. A closing forum features ways to alleviate stress and face reality without depending on drugs. Without emphasizing it or referring directly to Christianity, the forum also suggests that individuals have spiritual problems to which there can only be spiritual answers. Evangelism and depth politics come full circle.

Finally, and very much at the level of governmental politics, a state legislator who is a member of First Presbyterian is helped to see the drug problem in a new dimension. He finds his own consideration of bills pending on the subject enriched and deepened, and he is later able to attach some significant amendments. The drug scourge, of course, is not removed overnight. And First Presbyterian still has many tensions over political concerns. But there is progress, there is hope, and Mabs and her friends now see more of the fullness of the gospel.

Chapter 3

CAN I KNOW GOD'S WILL FOR MY LIFE?

David Neff

When CHRISTIANITY TODAY asked its readers which religious questions seemed important to them, "Does God have a plan for my life, and if so, am I living it?" received the second-highest number of "high interest" ratings—62 per cent of those surveyed. (More detailed results of the survey can be found on pages 9–10.)

The editors knew divine guidance was an important topic to young Christians. But when we considered that the average CT reader is in his or her forties, we were surprised at the high rating this question received. Not being content merely to warm up old wisdom on this subject, we decided to consider what the question of divine guidance means for persons in midlife.

Many religious people expend their spiritual energies telling God how much they love him and about the wonderful plan they have for *his* life. Of course, they don't put it that way, but—cloaked in proper pious platitudes—they devote their prayers to telling God what to do.

On the other hand, mature followers of Jesus Christ are more concerned about God's will for *their* lives. Thus they may spend more prayer time in listening than in talking.

But listening for God's voice has become a problem for many Christians. Some seem to hear his voice as perhaps Joan of Arc heard it, getting her instructions from Saints Michael, Catherine, and Margaret—and then they proceed to take on impossible and irrational projects just as the Maid of Orléans did. Others listen, if not exactly expecting to hear voices, at least hoping for some solid assurance that God wants them to choose a particular path at a crossroads in their lives. And when they don't get it, their faith may falter as they raise the wrong question: whether God is present in their lives, rather than whether some of the talk they have heard on guidance might not be a bit vacant. To add to the puzzlement, there are indeed some who listen faithfully, act on what they hear, and live lives of exemplary spiritual achievement.

Have I done well?

The puzzlement is unfortunately complicated for people who are reaching midlife. Much of the writing about knowing God's will for our lives has been focused on questions and spiritual approaches appropriate to youth.

After World War II came to an end, and as the United States was flooded by G.I.'s seeking jobs, educations, and sweethearts, Christian thinkers addressed the question of God's will largely in terms of choosing a career and finding a mate. Twenty years later, as the leading edge of the baby boom entered college, the concerns were largely the same. But in the last decade of the twentieth century, the boomer bulge is entering the bewildering landscape of "midlife crisis"—and facing a new series of questions.

While both young adults and midlife Christians are dealing with issues of identity, these Who-am-I questions take a different form at different stages of life. Young adults ask, "Who am I?" by asking which career to pursue or whether to pursue a career at all. Midlife adults are more likely to ask whether they have been successful in their chosen careers. Young adults try to understand their sexual future by asking whether they should marry and, if so, whom. Midlife adults are more likely to examine their sexual past, asking whether their earlier choices about marriage and children were indeed the right ones, and whether they have fulfilled their obligations and, in turn, been fulfilled by them. Young adults try to gain knowledge by earning degrees and honing their techniques. Midlifers, by contrast, try to consolidate wisdom by asking what they have learned.

The questions of midlife, thus, are essentially evaluations (Have I done well?), while the questions of young adulthood are choices (What shall I do?). This process of evaluation is an opportunity for growth as well as a door to disaster.

For example, giving a negative answer to the question "Have I paid enough attention to my children and instructed them well?" can help midlifers recognize shortcomings and do what they can to improve relations with their nearly grown offspring. But in some circumstances, it can call forth a neurotic response that imposes moralistic and restrictive religion on teenagers who are by now supposed to be discovering their own values and testing their own judgment.

Likewise, a sense of failure within marriage can lead to deepened intimacy and understanding. Or it can produce a panicky search for intimacy and excitement outside of marriage, resulting in the pain of separation, divorce, and child-support payments.

Unworkable ideas
Not only are the kinds of questions asked in midlife different, but the understandings that are often taught to young people of how God guides are no longer workable in a period of adjustment to imperfection and limits.

A number of erroneous ideas were at least tolerable in the energy of youth: (1) That missing God's preferred choice in a situation by choosing some other, but equally God-honoring and moral, path will lead to spiritual ruin. (2) That the special guidance given to apostles and prophets as they spread the Good News or corrected

God's people is somehow the norm for what all Christians should expect. (3) That God's scriptural revelation of right, of wrong, and of principles to live by is not sufficient information for us to please God.

Young people, who are more spiritually idealistic, energetic, and resilient, may survive this kind of erroneous teaching. But these ideas, if taken seriously at midlife, can be much more potent for spiritual ruin. Either midlifers will give up hope of special guidance and therefore give up hope in God, or they will listen to their subjectivity, follow their impulses, and claim God's blessing for the turmoil they create. In this regard, I never cease to be amazed at those who abandon hope for their marriages and pass through an illicit affair or two on their way to a second union, only to interpret that experience as God releasing them from bondage and bringing them a blessing in the guise of a new spouse. However unwise our early choices may have been, there is never an excuse for trying to improve the situation by violating the clear commands of Scripture.

Similarly, a number of curious practices commonly taught to young people can have disastrous effects in midlife: (1) Expecting private messages from Scripture, using the Bible as an oracle, expecting it to behave more like the I Ching than like what it is—the written record of God's word and deed in specific and concrete historical circumstances. (2) Casting lots or aping the doubting, foot-dragging example of Gideon by putting out "fleeces." (3) Waiting with a blank mind for God to bring a message into consciousness.

All of these spurious ideas and practices are essentially manifestations of distrust in God. It is in Scripture that God has given us clear instruction in righteousness and wisdom; he has given us wise counselors to help us apply it to our lives; and he has granted us the freedom to act within the boundaries of his will. To turn then to God and demand special guidance in decision making is to say, "I fear you and don't trust the gifts you have given me. I am afraid that if I make a mistake, you will reject me and I will face spiritual ruin."

Why ask?

Why then do we even bother ourselves about seeking God's plan for our lives? Why do we so often put ourselves through the anguish of searching? While all Christians wish to live within God's will, most of us proceed in our day-by-day routine doing the tasks we find at hand. We feel settled that it is God's will for us to change the baby's diapers, go to the office, mow the lawn, and teach our children well. We also know it is God's will that we not do certain things—lie to the Internal Revenue Service, for example, or sexually abuse children.

And we do not bother much to ask God about the incidental affairs of living. These questions we recognize as having no moral significance.

But as midlife adults, it is natural for us to ask about God's will for our lives partly because of what Scripture says, and partly because of what our psyches tell us.

The intimate God

Scripture tells us of a God who is near to us: one who keeps account of the hairs on our heads (Matt. 10:20; Luke 12:7); one who has plans for *some* of us from the moment of conception (Judges 13:5; Ps. 139:13–15; Jer. 1:5); one who wants good things for us in the same way a father wants good things for each of his children (Luke 11:11–13). God even keeps track of the two-for-a-farthing sparrows, Jesus said. Of how much more value are we human beings than birds to him (Matt. 10:29, 31; Luke 12:6–7)!

We could infer from these texts that God has a plan for us. How could an all-wise God who knows us better than we know ourselves not have a blueprint for our lives, an itinerary through the bewildering choices of career and job assignment, housing and community choice, mate and offspring? The fact that certain biblical characters were chosen before their births to do special work for God seems to reinforce this idea. And the mystical direction of the Spirit experienced by such as Paul and Philip (Acts 8:26–29; 13:1–7; 16:10, 6–7) likewise gives the impression that God has our lives mapped out for us.

But is that the necessary implication? Healthy parental love wishes for its offspring a rich and rewarding life. But healthy parental love does not force its specific hopes—that a daughter should marry a doctor, for example, or be one herself—on its children. Healthy parental love gives guidelines for safety. ("Don't stick your fingers in electric outlets," we tell our little ones, and when they're older, "Don't drink and drive, or accept a ride from those who do.") Wise parents try to inculcate good habits and edifying practices (brushing and flossing regularly, going to church and giving to charity, and changing your oil every three to four thousand miles). But within wise guidelines, our children face a creation that is bulging with good possibilities. And healthy parents encourage their offspring to invest themselves in those possibilities.

Likewise, God seems to have given our first parents only a few limitations ("Don't touch that tree, but from all the others you may *freely* eat") and a host of possibilities. And our spiritual ancestors received moral and spiritual laws (the Ten Commandments in particular and the Mosaic legislation in general) that guarded their heritage of "life, liberty, and the pursuit of happiness" (not strictly biblical terms, I realize, but not exactly unbiblical either).

Under the New Covenant, Christians are encouraged to live in a spirit of freedom and sonship rather than in a spirit of fear and slavery (Rom. 8:14–17; Gal. 4–5). In fact, without revoking any of his former guidelines, God has articulated for those who walk in the Spirit a summary guideline of sacrificial love; for those who live by a rule of self-sacrifice in search of the good of their fellow human beings will surely fulfill all of the moral and spiritual laws.

It seems from Scripture that God does on occasion have special purposes for chosen individuals. But it also appears from Scripture that the bulk of humanity is given the freedom and responsibility to choose wisely within the limits of the moral law. This has been argued briefly but cogently by J. I. Packer on the pages of *Eternity* (April, May, June 1986) and at length by Gary Friesen with J. Robin Maxson in their book *Decision Making and the Will of God: A Biblical Alternative to the Traditional View* (Multnomah Press, 1980). It seems only reasonable that to those creatures he has made in his image, God gives the principle and burden of freedom. The daunting truth about our high calling is well put by Bishop Dafyd in Stephen R. Lawhead's *Merlin* (Crossway, 1988): "The higher a man's call and vision, the more choices are given him. This is our work in creation: to decide. And what we decide is woven into the thread of time and being forever. Choose wisely, then, but you must choose" (p. 328).

The desperate search for God's favor

But despite God's gift of freedom, it seems that many people expect him to have an agenda for their existence, perhaps not because of what Scripture tells them, but because of what their psyches whisper. Of course, the desire to please God in making our choices great and small is a sign of spiritual health. But there is another drive to please—a desperate desire to pacify God and win his favor by divining exactly what he wants and doing only precisely that. That desire is a sign of spiritual pathology. This inability to live with uncertainty, to allow God to allow us freedom, may often be rooted in a bad experience with a parent or other authority figure. I have seen this consuming passion most often in people who felt abandoned by a parent—an adopted teen whose adoptive parents beat her; a collegiate man whose father died early and unexpectedly of cancer; another whose father still lived but had grown cold, distant, and uncommunicative. In counseling, all of these persons came to recognize that they subconsciously feared God would abandon them (as the human parents had) if they failed to win his favor at every juncture in their lives.

Midlife can bring this fear of abandonment even more intensely than young adulthood. And thus midlife anxieties can produce an even more intense search for being "in the will of God" as an assurance that when other aspects of life are decaying, at least one can Jacob-like tighten a full-nelson hold on God.

At midlife, many adults discover they are not going to rise any higher in their organizations. They discover they will probably never enter a higher salary bracket than they already have. They find their superiors at work noticing the industry, creativity, and stamina of younger employees—all at the very point when their own energies begin to ebb and their joints begin to stiffen. They discover their children are not achieving all they had hoped. And they realize their children are no longer malleable, but already set steadily on their own courses. They may find their own marriages have lost their luster and that, as the children grow older and leave home, the needs of offspring can no longer distract attention from deficiencies in their marriage. And then their friends and former classmates begin to die off, just one or two, in accidents or with untimely coronaries; but the person in midlife has entered the valley of the shadow of death.

Loss is real at this stage. Loss of goals. Loss of energy. Loss of a sense of accomplishment. Loss of family pride. Loss of friends. And loss of faith—for those who have been good churchgoing, pillar-of-the-community Christians discover that even their faithfulness to religion has not made them exceptions to the life patterns of the rest of humanity. As Raymond Studzinski writes:

> The desire to totally control one's environment and one's future, frequently through a close relationship with God, the all-good provider, has proven to be unrealizable. Plagued by unfulfilled dreams and by shattered ideals, persons at midlife find that the enemy of their fulfillment and happiness is less outside themselves in other people or in situations and more within, in their own hearts. They experience their internal chaos in terms of not knowing what they want, what they care for, or if anything is worthwhile. Rather than being fulfilled, they feel drained by all they have done in their lives. Life looks like a series of losses with the greatest loss, that of life itself, still ahead. (Raymond Studzinski, O.S.B., *Spiritual Direction and Midlife Development* [Chicago: Loyola University Press, 1985], p. 37).

Whenever a person is moving into a new phase of life it is not unusual for him or her to want to hold on to elements of the former stage. Every parent learns how a teenager can act remarkably mature one minute and revert to utter childishness the next. At least for the teen there is the promise of increased freedom and responsibility that will lure him or her to "put away childish things." But what is to motivate the person in middle age to move ahead developmentally? The promise of false teeth and bifocals? Thus it is only natural that the midlife person will try to grasp at the piety of his or her youth, longing for the excitement and enthusiasm that followed conversion and trying to revive the sense of God's intimacy that accompanied an important personal spiritual experience. But that energy cannot be contrived. A spiritual discovery once made cannot be made again. And thus the midlife adult often feels the loss of God's presence along with the loss of youth, idealism, and opportunity.

The most healthy reaction is not to look for God in an idealized past, but to move into the future, confident that God will present himself to us in new and different ways.

For example, the believer who does not try to recreate his or her spiritual past can find God's presence and a sense of direction in different scriptural stories and motifs from the ones that appealed in the passionate and energetic days of youth. Teens and college students are often challenged by images of the young Daniel and his friends standing firm for truth in the court schools of Babylon. Or perhaps they are inspired by the exploits of a young Gideon, David, or Esther. Stories of courage and accomplishment are models for the channeling of the spiritual energies of the young in the service of God. But the midlife believer, who sees that his tomorrows are fewer than his yesterdays, and who realistically comes to understand that many of his earlier goals may now be unreachable, will find inspiration in the biblical tales of failure, of repentance, and of persistence: Peter's rebounding from faithlessness to take a post of apostolic leadership; Paul's wisdom and faithfulness in spite of the physical torment of his "thorn in the flesh" and the politicization of the churches he had helped found; Hosea's faithfulness in the face of Gomer's promiscuity; the aging David's acceptance of his inability to complete the building of the temple, yet doing what he could to amass the materials. These stories can be inspirations at midlife.

Similarly, persons in midlife must look for God's presence and listen for his direction in the new challenges that come with a new phase of living. Many midlife men, for example, are given a new opportunity in the workplace. Instead of being rising young stars who must demonstrate their abilities and pursue the goal of career advancement, midlife men often find they have risen nearly as far as they will go in the corporate structure. The opportunity then presents itself to become a mentor, to take the skills, wisdom, and savvy acquired in the first 20 years of work life, and use them to help younger, more energetic workers to develop themselves and make a contribution to their field. Thus one can find God's presence in these new serving relationships.

And more than ever, midlife persons can seek God's presence and guidance in their relationships with fellow believers. The achievement-oriented lives of so many young adults effectively prevent them from developing deep relationships in either the family or the church. So much energy and time is devoted to making it financially and achieving advancement that barely enough is left for perfunctory family meals and church attendance. But midlife can be a time of consolidation rather than expansion. Wise midlifers may recognize that they have reached a career plateau. For these individuals, the pressure is off if they will allow themselves to be thankful for what they have achieved with God's help. If they will, they can then turn their attentions to mining the riches of their relationships. And in these relationships, they can find God's presence and his guidance.

A few years before I formally became a midlifer (the transition begins at about age 40 and ends at about 45, says Studzinski), I was considering a career change. Should I return to school for a degree in clinical psychology? I asked myself. After all, I had done a fair amount of pastoral counseling, something I had enjoyed. I asked God for guidance, and then asked four Christian friends who knew me well: a former student who had graded papers for me; a former secretary who was now involved in career guidance counseling; a fellow campus minister with whom I shared racquetball games and locker-room chat twice a week; and my wife. All four said it would be the wrong choice—and each of them gave different reasons. And all the reasons were compelling. Later, when I considered becoming an editor, the voices of friends confirmed the decision. At all stages of our lives, God makes himself present to us in our relationships. But at midlife, we need to turn to our friends more than ever. And in addition, we need to avail ourselves of the spiritual mentors God has placed at our disposal in the church.

Love for the unlovely
Understanding two aspects of the character of God is important to the person in midlife, for these scriptural themes help us feel yet more comfortable in our relationship with God at the same time they help us make decisions consistent with God's character.

First, God is characterized by covenant faithfulness. So, too, should his people be. If there is any aspect of God's character that through sheer repetition in the Hebrew Scriptures should impress us, it is this characteristic. The Hebrew word *chesedh* appears nearly 250 times in Scripture—mostly in connection with God's character. Often translated "lovingkindness" and still more often "mercy" in the older translations, when associated with divine love the word is perhaps best rendered as "covenant faithfulness." Or as E. M. Good writes, *chesedh* is "a faithful love, a steadfast, unshakable mainte-nance of the covenantal relationship" ("Love in the OT," *The Inter-preter's Dictionary of the Bible*, vol. 3, p. 167).

The steadiness of God's covenant love is spotlighted repeatedly by the unfaithfulness of Israel. In spite of their whoring after other gods, their syncretistic adaptations of pagan deities, and their grinding the faces of the poor, Yahweh's lovingkindness seems to endure forever. He continues to send his messengers, the prophets, to woo them and warn them.

The biblical covenant between Yahweh and his people has both a unilateral and a bilateral character. It is radically one-sided, of course, for Yahweh chooses a group of people who have little to recommend them, leads them forth from bondage, gives them civil and moral laws by which to live, gives them food and drink, and finally, he gives them a land in which to live. All this he does when they are so disorganized and disorderly they cannot hope to take any credit themselves. Thus his covenant with them, his agreement or contract, is one-sided. They have little to do but accept his terms. To be holy as he is holy (Exod. 19:5–6), to remain within his covenant and keep his commands (Exod. 20:6; Deut. 5:10). Knowing their weakness, however, Yahweh promises to be faithful.

Yet there is a subtle two-sidedness here. While Yahweh knows their weakness, while he realistically understands that he will not receive perfect obedience from this nation newly formed, he places upon them the condition of keeping covenant, that is, to remember him as the source of their existence (Deut. 6:10–15), to obey his commands (Deut. 7:6–11), and to be holy as he is holy (Lev. 11:45). After all, as David sings in 2 Samuel 22:26, with those who are faithful, God is faithful ("With the *chasidh* you practice *chesedh*").

Christian theologians differ on whether God's covenant love for Israel is in some way conditioned on their continued obedience. A case can be made from Scripture for the idea that God's covenant faithfulness has its limits. And a case can be made for the completely unlimited character of that *chesedh*. But biblical scholars of all kinds will agree that God's covenant faithfulness includes a toler-ance far beyond any human comprehension.

Human covenants are by their nature more bilateral than divine covenants. But the promises we make (as in the marriage service) and the promises inherent in our very existence (as in our relationships to our children) are to be characterized by a divinely unilateral quality. No matter what my children may do, they are still my children. No matter what my spouse may do, she is still spouse to me. Wise Christians therefore treat these bonds as indissoluble. And in the turmoil of midlife, they preserve these covenant relationships by practicing a longsuffering lovingkindness.

Faithful in the face of failure

The painful story of Hosea and his fidelity to the faithless Gomer is recorded in Scripture as a parable of God's utter faithfulness and an example of how human love can partake of divine *chesedh*. In the face of Israel's spiritual adultery, God says he will romance her: "Therefore"—that is, because of Israel's idolatry (Gomer's adultery)—"therefore, behold, I will allure her, and bring her into the wilderness, and speak tenderly to her. . . . And there she shall answer as in the days of her youth as at the time when she came out of the land of Egypt. . . . And I will betroth you to me for ever; I will betroth you to me in righteousness and in justice, in steadfast love [*chesedh*] and in mercy. I will betroth you to me in faithfulness; and you shall know the LORD" (Hosea 2:14, 15b, 19–20).

The word of the Lord through Hosea is the word of faithfulness in the face of infidelity. When midlife Christians evaluate the "success" of their relationships, they must remember that God, who condemns his people's idolatry, lives yet by his covenant with them.

It is natural for persons in midlife to evaluate the health and success of their relationships. But midlife Christians must resist the temptation to write off completely the relationship that did not fulfill their romantic (and perhaps unreasonable) expectations. Seeking solace or excitement in an affair is anything but practicing covenant faithfulness. Love does not seek solace; love does not thrive on thrills. Love suffers; love forgives; love nurtures; and love heals when possible. And rather than discarding a relationship, love examines it to see whether it might be entering a new chapter of existence. But to try to discover a divine excuse for infidelity by saying it was God who brought you and your paramour together is ludicrous. God's will for all Christian lives is a lifetime of covenant faithfulness.

Such covenant faithfulness is difficult, to be sure. But it can indeed be rewarding—even when a divorce seems inevitable.

Divorce certainly seemed inevitable when Ellen returned from a trip abroad. Charles could tell from her distant coolness that something had changed for the worse and that the marriage was over. That was over five years ago. Charles still doesn't know if Ellen was unfaithful to him on that trip. But whatever had happened had caused Ellen to turn on him and blame him for all her bad experiences and turbulent emotions. Charles, hurt though he was, decided to exercise covenant faithfulness, to act like a husband even though Ellen wouldn't let him be a husband. Over the next few years, Charles insisted that she see a counselor and face her inner turmoil; he insisted that they come to an agreement about their property and avoid expensive and upsetting legal wrangles; he helped Ellen get launched on a new career (she now makes significantly more than his ministerial salary); and when she wanted to save money for a down payment on a new house for herself and their son, he invited her to move back in with him so she could set the money aside. Over five years passed between their separation and their divorce, but those five years were a time of growth for both and, in a curious kind of way, faithfulness for Charles. Ellen's midlife turmoil could have spelled emotional and financial disaster for them both. Charles's Hosea-like commitment avoided ruin even when he could not single-handedly avoid divorce.

To be godlike at midlife means to hold faithfully on course, as Charles did, even when faced with failure. But Charles's story also demonstrates another aspect of God's character.

The chess master
God is the master of creative possibilities, one who is not boxed in by our bad choices. Having been created in his image, we share in that creativity. Surely Charles would have chosen another course for his ill-fated marriage; but given the realities of a sin-ripped world, Charles chose a creative path that wrung more good out of a painful situation than anyone might have hoped for. Likewise, the sovereign God (who is all wise) would often have chosen a course different from those chosen by his people through the ages. But given the hard realities of human history, the creative God finds ways to bring

victory from tragedy, success from failure, and hope from disappointment.

Einstein reputedly said, "God doesn't play dice." True, but I believe God does play chess. The essence of dice is chance; but the essence of chess is strategy; and the essence of strategy is looking beyond the narrow confines of the immediate challenge to the multitude of options that are open beyond. Human beings often feel squeezed by the either/or-ness of daily life. We may feel we have a narrow range of options, none of them particularly attractive. But like a good chess player, our sovereign God in his foreknowledge sees his second, third, and fourth moves hence. Thus he can—and does—bring good out of evil. This is illustrated in the wisdom of Joseph, who had been betrayed by his jealous brothers only to be made governor of Egypt. In Genesis 50, Joseph faces his fearful brothers and says, "You meant evil against me; but God meant it for good, to bring it about that many people should be kept alive, as they are today" (v. 20). No one could have advised those foolish brothers that it was God's will that they sell their sibling into slavery. But it was God's will that many should be preserved from starvation; and, like a chess master, he took the deplorable circumstances of Joseph's life and brought good to many. This must be the meaning of Romans 8:28, "We know that in everything God works for good with those who love him, who are called according to his purpose." It is not that Paul affirms the goodness of all circumstances, but that he affirms God's creative good will in all circumstances.

Can Christians find a way to be creatively godlike when faced with hard choices? Yes; they can choose not to follow their flesh-bound instincts and sulk, rebel, or give up. Instead, they can follow the intuitions of God's Spirit, which leads us to "be imitators of God," to "walk in love, as Christ loved us and gave himself up for us, a fragrant offering and sacrifice to God" (Eph. 5:1–2).

What gives us the courage to act in sacrificial and creative love, in unorthodox (by the world's standards) ways as Charles did in his disappointment with Ellen? It is the surety of God's faithful and creative love. When we love creatively, we can and do make mistakes. But we gain the courage to act from knowing that our mistakes are more than matched by God's creative opportunities. Nothing we do in the spirit of sacrificial love can permanently thwart his good and loving purpose for us.

Chapter 4

IS THE CHARISMATIC RENEWAL SEEN IN MANY CHURCHES TODAY, FROM GOD?

J. I. Packer

Some Christian leaders have called the charismatic renewal "demonic," while others have belittled it as mere emotionalism. At the other extreme are those who view it as the sole answer to the apathy and institutionalism that paralyze the church. CHRISTIANITY TODAY asked J. I. Packer, author of Keeping in Step with the Spirit *(Revell, 1984), to give us a brief but careful look at this movement that provokes such strong reactions.*

To ask this question (which was asked of CHRISTIANITY TODAY readers just as stated above) is like asking whether motor vehicles, seen on American roads today, are efficient. In each case the true answer doubtless is: In some respects yes, in others no. But both questions are too broad and unfocused for that answer to get us very far. If all we want to know is whether American "wheels" ordinarily work, as distinct from refusing to function, or whether God ordinarily blesses where the movement called charismatic renewal takes root, a simple "yes" will suffice, for that is in truth the fact. But if our goal is to assess how well American cars are built from the standpoint of safety, or fuel economy, or long life, or how mature and God-honoring charismatic patterns of godliness are as compared with alternative forms, past and present, some discussion is needed. I shall now discuss.

Behind our question lie two extremes of opinion. Some Christians pan the renewal as Ralph Nader used to pan American cars (remember *Unsafe at Any Speed*?). These critics dismiss charismatic distinctives as psychological or demonic, that is, self-induced or devised by the Devil, and tell us that embracing these distinctives is always spiritually stultifying and retrograde. Others applaud the renewal in what might be called Star Wars terms, seeing it as God's final triumphant move for preserving the church and spreading the gospel in today's anti-Christian world. Mediating assessments fan out between these two extremes. Where does biblical wisdom lead us to position ourselves on this spectrum? That is what we must try to see.

What is the charismatic movement?
First, let us make sure that we know what we are talking about. The charismatic movement, also called the renewal movement and the charismatic renewal, is a worldwide phenomenon some 30 years old. Some refer to it as the second Pentecostal wave, in distinction from the first wave that produced the Pentecostal denominations at the start of this century. It emerged in California, as did its predecessor, and has touched most Christian bodies, including the Roman Catholic community. Pentecostals are relatively unaffected, but that is natural since, from their standpoint, charismatic renewal is just the rest of the church catching up with what they themselves have

known for two generations. Intensively fertilized by interchange of leaders and lay personnel internationally, and by a flood of reading matter focused on charismatic distinctives, the movement has spread far and fast. An educated guess is that something like 25 million Christians outside the Pentecostal churches have grafted onto the basics of evangelical belief (by which I mean the message of ruin, redemption, and regeneration, and of personal trust in Christ as one's crucified, risen, reigning, and returning Savior) a recognizably charismatic approach to Christian and church life.

What is that approach? It is a matter of embracing some, if not all, of the following items:

1. A hermeneutical claim that all elements of New Testament ministry and experience may with propriety be hoped for, sought, and expected today, none of them having permanently ceased when the apostolic age ended.

2. An empirical claim that among the elements of New Testament ministry and experience now enjoyed within the renewal are (i) experiential postconversion Spirit-baptism, as seen in Acts 2:1–4; 8:14–17; 10:44–46 with 11:15–17; 19:1–6; (ii) tongues, understood as glossolalia (uttering languagelike sounds) rather than xenolalia (speaking languages one never learned) and as given primarily for private devotional use; (iii) interpretation of tongues, when spoken in public; (iv) prophecy, understood as receiving and relaying messages directly from God; (v) miraculous healing through prayer; (vi) deliverance from demonic influences through exorcism; and (vii) words of knowledge, understood as supernatural disclosings of information about individuals to those who seek to minister to their needs.

3. A high valuation of one's own glossolalia as a personal prayer language, and deliberate frequent use of it.

4. Emphasis on the church as the body of Christ, upheld and led on to maturity by the Holy Spirit through the mutual love and supernaturally empowered service of its members.

5. A concern to identify and harness each Christian's spiritual gift or gifts for body-ministry.

6. Insistence that worship is central in the church's common life, and that the heart and climax of true worship is united praise as distinct from preaching and Eucharist (which have been the historic

focal centers of Protestant and Roman Catholic worship respectively).

7. The cultivation of a relaxed, leisurely, intimate, informal style of corporate worship, aimed at evoking feelings of awe and joy before the Lord and at expressing love and loyalty to him for his saving grace.

8. The use for this purpose of simple, repetitive choruses and "renewal songs," often consisting of biblical texts set to music in a modern folk idiom for performance with guitar accompaniment. Guitars may be reinforced by melody instruments and also by tambourines, bongos, and jazz drums, as in a dance band's rhythm section.

9. The congregational practice of "singing in the Spirit"—that is, sustaining ad lib, and moving within, the full-close chord with which a hymn or song ends, vocalizing extemporarily and some-times glossolalically in the process.

10. Encouragement of physical expression of the spirit of praise and prayer by raising hands, swinging the body, dancing, prostrat-ing oneself, and other such gestures. Bodily movements of this kind are held to deepen worship by intensifying the mood being expressed, and thus to glorify God.

11. Expectation of prophecy in worship gatherings, either as an immediate on-the-spot message from God or as the remembered fruit of a vision or a dream, and the provision of opportunity to utter it to the congregation.

12. The typical perception of people both outside and inside the community of faith less as guilty sinners than as moral, spiritual, and emotional cripples, scarred, soured, and desperately needing deliverance from bondages in their inner lives; and the structuring of counseling and prayer ministries to meet their need, thus viewed.

13. The practice of prayer with laying on of hands, for all who desire it, as a regular conclusion to worship gatherings. Those who are sick, disabled, and troubled in mind are particularly urged to receive this ministry, and to expect benefit through it.

14. A counseling technique of leading pained, grieved, inhibited, and embittered souls to visualize Christ and involve him therapeuti-cally in the reliving of their traumatic hurts, as a means to inner healing.

15. A confident assumption that it is not ordinarily God's will

that any of his children should continue in pain, or in any mental and emotional state other than joy, and a consequent downplaying of the older Christian stress on the spiritual benefit of humbly accepted suffering.

16. An insistent claim that miraculous-looking "signs and wonders" (especially "healings") have evidential value that will convince modern Westerners of the truth and power of the gospel, and that "signs and wonders" should therefore be sought from God by prayer in each congregation.

17. A firm belief that some, if not all, disturbed people with addictive enslavements (bondages) are under the influence of demons who must be detected and exorcised.

18. A commitment to aggressive evangelism, aimed at inducing the self-willed to repent and open their lives to Jesus Christ and his Holy Spirit.

19. Emphasis on the benefit of communal and community living; of prayerfully sharing all one's concerns with "the body," normally in small groups, and of accepting discipline and guidance from other Christians in authoritative mentor relationships.

20. Insistence that established patterns of personal and church life must always be open to change so that Holy Spirit life may find freer expression, and expectation that all Christians, fellowships, and congregations will need to make such change over and over again.

21. Expectant openness to divine guidance by prophecy, vision, and dreams.

22. Confidence that a shared charismatic experience and lifestyle unifies Protestants and Roman Catholics at a deeper level than that at which doctrine divides them.

23. A devotional temper of exuberant euphoria, expressing a sense of loving intimacy with the Father and the Son that has in it little self-assessment and self-criticism, but is affectionate and adoring in a happily childlike way.

From all angles
How should we bring this kaleidoscopic phenomenon into focus? Evaluation needs to be made from a number of angles.

Sociologically, the charismatic movement is a restrained white middle-class reinvention of original working-class, black-style, "holy roller" Pentecostalism, from which, unobtrusively and perhaps unconsciously, it has borrowed much of its theology. Its relative uninhibitedness frequently approaches, but rarely transgresses, the bounds of educated good taste, and its verbal and behavioral style evidently intends to remain within those bounds.

Spiritually, it is a recognizable mutation of the Bible-based conversionist piety fostered in seventeenth-century Puritanism, in New England's Great Awakening, and old England's Evangelical Revival in the eighteenth century, and in the nineteenth-century Protestant missionary movement—the type of piety that is nowadays labeled "evangelical." Original Pentecostalism was an adaptation of this piety in its Wesleyan form, but Calvinistic charismatics are currently found in some strength.

Doctrinally, the renewal is in the mainstream of historic evangelical orthodoxy on the Trinity, the Incarnation, the objectivity of Christ's Atonement and the historicity of his Resurrection, the need of regeneration by the Holy Spirit, personal fellowship with the Father and the Son as central to the life of faith, and the divine truth of the Bible to go no further. There is nothing eccentric about its basic teaching.

Culturally, the charismatic movement appears as a child of our time in its antitraditionalism; its anti-intellectualism; its romantic emotionalism in expressing love, to God as to human beings; its desire for thrills and for the ability to live always on an emotional high; its narcissistic preoccupation with physical health and ease of mind; its preference for folk-type music with poetically uncouth lyrics (the uncouthness arguing sincerity in the modern manner); and its cultivated informality. In all these respects, the renewal reflects the late twentieth-century Western world back at itself.

Theologically, charismaticism is a mixed bag, as witnesses this perceptive vignette by Richard Lovelace:

> The charismatic renewal continues to express the mystical spirituality of the Puritan and awakening eras, but often without the rational and theological checks against error and credulity maintained by evangelicals. As a consequence, charismatics have some of the problems of the radical

spiritualists in the anabaptist and Puritan left wing. Gifts of
the Spirit are more prominent than the call to sanctification. The charismatic garden has a luxuriant overgrowth of
theological weeds, including the health-and-wealth gospel,
the most virulent form of the American heresy that Christianity guarantees worldly success. A fuzzy and unstruc-
tured ecumenism lives side by side with rampant sectari-
anism" ("Evangelical Spirituality: A Church Historian's
Perspective," *Journal of the Evangelical Theological Society*,
31:1, March 1988, p. 33).

Granted, the renewal has an enviable track record of enlivening
the spiritually dead and energizing the spiritually paralyzed, but
whether it commands the resources to lead them on to full-orbed
Christian maturity is another matter. When the liturgical and
pastoral innovations that originally channel the new life become
routines as stylized as those they replaced, and the limitations listed
by Lovelace are accepted as normal, is not some writing beginning
to appear on the wall? And the question, How may the renewal be
renewed?, does not seem to have been faced as yet, let alone
answered.

Not from God?
But even if the charismatic movement has no more to give to the
church than it has given already, it is surely strange that it should
ever be dismissed as not "from God"—that is, as manifesting
throughout something other than God's grace, so that every element
of it should be explained as merely human or actually demonic. Yet
that verdict has on occasion been voiced. How should we respond?
  Our first comment must be that such thinking is largely emotional
and irrational. The human mind has an unhappy tendency to jump
from specifics we dislike to blanket condemnations of the larger
reality of which the specifics are part. Someone misbehaves once, so
we tag him as a no-good forever. We think a retail store cheated us
over one purchase, so we resolve never to shop there again. Our car
gives trouble, so we henceforth refuse all cars of that make. So, too, if
charismatic phenomena offend our sense of social, liturgical, or
theological propriety, and charismatic individuals embarrass us
and make us feel threatened, we are very apt to respond by abusing

the whole movement and denying that there is anything of God in it at all. But how silly! And how nasty! This is a reaction of wounded pride and willful prejudice, and as such is bad thinking in every way.

Our second comment must be that by biblical standards the negative verdict is impossible. This can be seen from an argument classically set out by Jonathan Edwards in the aftermath of the much-criticized Great Awakening, of which he became the prime defender. In *The Distinguishing Marks of a Work of the Spirit of God*, Edwards reasons as follows: Any movement that (1) exalts Jesus Christ as Son of God and Savior, leading people to honor him as such; (2) opposes Satan's kingdom by weaning people from sin and worldliness; (3) teaches people to revere and trust the Bible as the Word of God; (4) makes people feel the urgency of eternal issues and the depth of their own lostness without Christ; and (5) stirs up in people new love of Christ and of others must be a divine work at its heart, whatever disfigurements may appear on its surface, since these are effects that Satan and fallen mankind have no wish to induce, and in fact try to avoid. But the Great Awakening had these distinguishing marks; therefore it was a work of God.

That the charismatic renewal has had the same fivefold effect is beyond dispute; therefore, it too must be adjudged a work of God. No doubt human folly breaks surface in it, as happens in all movements involving human excitement; no doubt Satan, whose nature and purpose is always to spoil any good God produces, keeps pace with God in it, engineering lunatic fanaticism within its ranks as he did in the Great Awakening. But to diagnose human and Satanic disfigurements of this contemporary work of God is altogether different from seeing it as intrinsically the fruit of psychological freakiness or Satanic malice.

Our third comment must be that aspects of the renewal raise real theological problems that should not be ignored or glossed over, even if the movement as a whole is given a relatively clean bill of health. We need to reflect on some of these:

1. Charismatics sometimes claim that their distinctive doctrines are proved true by the blessing that God gives through the teaching of them and the ministry based upon them. This, however, is a mistake. Because God is gracious, those who seek him with their whole hearts find his blessing even if their thoughts about that

blessing are, and remain, askew. The deadening effect of views that keep people from seeking blessings that are there for them (for instance, medieval teaching on faith, which by telling folk to trust themselves to the church stopped them from seeking assured forgiveness from Christ's own hand) is obvious; but that is not the problem here. If charismatics err, they err only by expecting to receive from God, whose face they seek, more than he has actually promised. Whether the expectations of charismatics are biblically realistic and whether they really receive what they expect are open questions, but the certainty that God meets and blesses all who seek him in honest and hearty prayer is beyond all question. Scripture is explicit on that (see 2 Chron. 7:14; 15:2, 12–15; Ps. 9:10; 24:3–6; 27:7–14; 70:4; 119:2, 58; Prov. 8:17; Jer. 29:13; Matt. 6:33; 7:7–11). Striking answers to humble prayers do not, however, guarantee that one's understanding of God's promises is correct, or that God means these striking answers to become the rule rather than remain the exception.

2. Sharing charismatic experience is often declared, as we noted earlier, to unify Protestants and Roman Catholics at a deeper level than that at which their doctrine divides them. This, if so, gives charismaticism great ecumenical significance, but for some the mere making of such a claim destroys the credibility of the renewal as a work of God. I am, myself, a Protestant who finds the official papacy and its trappings grotesque, and official Roman Catholic teaching on the church's infallible authority, on the Mass, and on Mary grossly and grievously mistaken, and therefore I sympathize with those for whom this charismatic claim demonstrates that at its heart the renewal is unspiritual and blind. But I do not accept the critics' assumption that if the love and reverence for Scripture that charismatic experience evokes was truly from God it would lead Romanists to question these doctrines and the system that maintains them in the way that Protestants do. Everyone observes that Protestant charismatics are concerned for the church ("the body") not as a confessing and theologizing institution, but as a worshiping and serving fellowship. And we also observe that the renewal among Protestants is a pietistic phenomenon, interdenominational because undenominational, concerned, first, with the spiritual life that flows from a living relationship to each person of the godhead in saving

grace, and, second, with fruitful fellowship and outreach on the part of those who have thus come to life. Unsurprisingly, the same is true of Roman Catholics. They had their reasons for being Roman before they met the renewal, and part of the Catholic package is that the institutional church has the last and decisive word in biblical interpretation, so that using Scripture to challenge church teaching is off limits. So one should not treat the failure of renewed Roman Catholics to mount such a challenge as evidence that their experience, and the movement that midwifed it, are somehow spiritually phony.

The truth is that charismatic ecumenism, if we are to call it that (and many do), is a limited and truncated thing, just because charismatics put all their energy into transdenominational concerns and leave questions of official church teaching and structures on one side. I personally believe that developing a shared spirituality is far and away the most constructive and necessary form of ecumenical action that can be taken in the world church today. But that does not mean that charismatic renewal constitutes a full-orbed ecumenism just because it majors in spirituality. Someday in the future, divergences of belief between and within churches will have to be discussed again; they present issues that cannot be shelved indefinitely. In the meantime, however, the fact that the professedly Bible-based renewal shelves church questions should not be held to destroy its claim to be a genuine work of God, embodying and projecting for popular consumption a significant form of ecumenical piety. That claim must be decided on other grounds.

3. The charismatic insistence that what are sometimes called "sign-gifts" (tongues and interpretation, healing gifts, prophecy, words of wisdom and knowledge) are still given, with its corollary that those who do not seek them miss something important, raises problems. Paul speaks of "signs, wonders and miracles" as "things that mark an apostle" (2 Cor. 12:12). Hebrews 2:3–4 speaks of them as confirming the apostles' testimony, and the Book of Acts knows them only in connection with the apostles' personal ministry. The common assumption that God withdrew the "sign-gifts" after the apostolic age cannot, perhaps, be proved, but it cannot be disproved, either. It is gratuitous to take for granted that every form of God's

working in New Testament times is meant to be reproduced today: Who among us nowadays raises the dead? And comparisons of contemporary charismatic phenomena with their alleged New Testament prototypes is inconclusive. New Testament tongues were used in public, and there is no single unambiguous statement that they were ever used any other way (the supposition that Paul used tongues in private prayer, which is sometimes read into 1 Corinthians 14:18, cannot be read out of it). But charismatics value their tongues as a private prayer language. Can they, then, be an identical manifestation? Again, it cannot be made plausible that New Testament interpretation of tongues and prophecy corresponded exactly to the phenomena that go by those names today, nor is it at all likely that the "word" ("message," NIV) of wisdom and knowledge in 1 Corinthians 12:8 corresponded to the (apparently) sanctified telepathy that goes by those names today. And the immediate, organic, large-scale, and uniformly successful healings ascribed to Christ and the apostles in the New Testament are certainly not matched by the frequently abortive efforts of present-day Christians with healing ministries. The claim that the apostolic "sign-gifts" continue is thus more than can be proved, and the verdict that charismatic manifestations are from God can only be reached by first acknowledging that they have no exact New Testament precedent and then judging them on the basis of their effect on people's moral and spiritual lives. Charismatics need to recognize this. (I have been here applying the principle insisted on by Edwards in his *Thoughts on the Revival.* I have discussed "sign-gifts" more fully in *Keep in Step with the Spirit,* pp. 200–34.)

4. Charismatics view Spirit baptism as a necessary postconversion experience, which God always models on the apostles' experience recorded in Acts 2:1–4 and identifies to its latter-day recipients by the gift of glossolalia. This thesis, borrowed from mainstream Pentecostalism, also raises problems.

What is at issue is not whether the Holy Spirit initiates and sustains states of mind in believers in which the love of the Father and the Son, the power of the Spirit himself, and the reality of spiritual evil are vividly grasped. Not only Pentecostal-charismatic accounts of Spirit baptism, but all mainstream Christian accounts of "infused" communion with God are given in these terms, and believers of all traditions follow the lead of the Psalms in asking God to grant and deepen this kind of experience. Nor is the issue whether the Spirit ever bestows mountain-peak moments of assurance, or ever induces glossolalia by his loving pressure upon us; we know, or should know, that on occasion he does both, and sometimes (not always) simultaneously.

What is in question is precisely this: whether Luke's narrative of Pentecost is teaching us that Christians who lack one such momentary experience, marked by tongues, are second-rate and not fully filled with the Holy Spirit, whatever else they may have experienced and done; or, putting it differently, whether Acts 2:1–4 is a revealed experiential norm for us all, as official Pentecostalism affirms. Against the claim that it is, I bring the following arguments:

(i) This is nowhere stated or implied in Acts, nor anywhere else in Scripture.

(ii) The claim is inconsistently made by those who make it. If the apostles spoke known languages at their Pentecost, why is not the same expected of us at ours? On what basis is glossolalia, which is not the speaking of known languages, accepted as a substitute? And why is not hearing a tornado sound and seeing fiery tongues, as the apostles did, required as part of the prescribed experience? If Acts 2:1–4 is to be taken strictly as the norm of Spirit baptism, no one today experiences Spirit baptism at all. If, however, the postconversion experience of God's integrating and empowering love through Christ, to which so many testify, is to be called Spirit baptism, as being somewhat like the apostles' experience on Pentecost morning, then Acts 2:1–4 is not strictly a norm—only a case of partial similarity. But if that is so, it would be better not to label this particular Christian experience "Spirit baptism" at all. Used thus unbiblically, the label can only confuse.

(iii) The reason why the apostles' experience of the new covenant ministry of the Spirit began at Pentecost, well after they came to faith, was not personal but dispensational. It had nothing to do with the quality or specific acts of their previous discipleship, but with the dawning of a new era of human enjoyment of God's grace here on Earth. Nowhere in the world was the Spirit's new covenant ministry operative till nine o'clock on Pentecost morning. The apostles' two-stage experience was thus unique to themselves, and is not a norm for us. The New Testament norm is stated in Peter's Pentecost sermon: All who believe and repent receive the Holy Spirit in the fullness of his enhanced ministry right at the outset (Acts 2:38). In line with this, Paul refers to Spirit-baptism as one aspect of our initiation into Christ at conversion (1 Cor. 12:13), and insists that all who are Christ's have the Spirit from the start (Rom. 8:9).

(iv) Acts 4:8, 31; 6:3, 5; 7:55; 9:17; 11:24; 13:9, and 52 all speak of persons being filled with, or full of, the Spirit, with no reference to tongues as accompanying that fullness. But if some were Spirit-filled without glossolalia then, some may also be now.

(v) Luke records four cases of "pentecostal" manifestations—one involving Jesus' disciples (Acts 2:1–4), one involving Samaritans (8:14–17), one involving gentile "God-fearers" (10:44–47), and one involving Ephesian followers of John the Baptist (19:1–7). The design of Acts makes it natural to think that he does this to exhibit God's acceptance on equal footing in the church of four different groups whose togetherness in Christ might otherwise have been doubted. Nothing suggests that his purpose is to establish norms of complete Christian experience for all; the impression left, rather, is that these manifestations were exceptional signs from God, not matched in the experience of other believers. Certainly, the burden of proof rests on anyone who would argue the contrary.

While believing, then, that through the Spirit many Christians experience intense moments of joyful assurance, and glossolalia becomes for some an authentic mode of praise and prayer, I reject the opinion that Acts 2:1–4 exhibits an experience that every Christian needs, and that God calls every Christian to seek, promising that those who seek will find; and by the same token I reject the view that those who cannot testify to this experience necessarily live on a lower plane than those who can.

Test everything
Now we must draw the threads together.

The charismatic renewal has brought millions of Christians, including many clergy, to a deeper, more exuberant faith in Christ than they had before. It has quickened thousands of congregations, invigorating their worship, making love and fellowship blossom among them, increasing their expectancy and enterprise, and giving a fillip to their evangelism. Charismatic insistence on openness to God has transformed countless lives that previously were not open to him. Is this from God? The question answers itself.

The pride and folly of triumphalism and the schismatic temper threaten the movement constantly, however, and need to be watched against unceasingly. Some things in the renewal are magnificent, but others are not right yet, and the liveliest Christian movements are naturally the objects of Satan's most diligent attention.

Some attitudes to the renewal, however, among Christians not involved in it, are not right either, and Satan loves to lure Christians into opposing the work of God. So the word in season to Christians both inside and outside the charismatic movement would seem to be: "Do not put out the Spirit's fire.... Test everything. Hold on to the good. Avoid every kind of evil.... The grace of our Lord Jesus Christ be with you" (1 Thess. 5:19–22, 28, NIV). Let all the people say, Amen!

Chapter 5

SHOULD WE EXPECT MIRACLES TODAY?

Colin Brown

Every few decades, with nearly the predictability of death and taxes, some Christian leader rediscovers the miraculous aspect of the New Testament and proclaims that miracles—usually healing miracles— should attend the church today.

In our own time, we have heard this teaching from classic Pentecostalism (represented most audibly by Oral Roberts), the charismatic movement in mainline churches, and from proponents of the "Third Wave of the Holy Spirit" (a term coined by missiologist C. Peter Wagner).

Christians in the more sedate churches are both puzzled by this teaching and intrigued by reports of spectacular healings, visions, and—occasionally—resurrections. Here theologian Colin Brown, author of two books on miracles, addresses the question: Should we expect miracles today?

Should we go?" The question floored me. If she had asked me the date of the Exodus, the finer points of the Arian controversy, or the issues involved in logical positivism, I could have spoken for an hour or two. But the mother who asked me the question was not interested in such topics. She was worried about her daughter and her medical problem. She was asking whether she should take her to the healing service held in the church down the road.

Although this happened 30 years ago, the memory of it is fresh. I had been ordained barely a month before. I was in my first pastorate, serving in a group of churches in the English Midlands. For the past three years I had been cramming my head with answers to all kinds of intellectual questions in order to get my theological degree. But the one question I was not ready for was "Should we expect biblical miracles today?"

As the weeks went by, I began to think more deeply about healing and miracles. I read books. I attended meetings. I got to know the minister who held the healing services. "You are only preaching half the gospel," he used to say, "if you are only preaching about forgiveness and salvation. When Jesus was on Earth, he healed as well as taught. He does the same today."

Thirty years later, I keep hearing the same challenge. But now—as then—I keep running into the same problems. The minister who held the healing services insisted that people were regularly being healed. But when I asked members of the staff of his church whether they had seen anything they would claim to be a miracle, they were more guarded. The conversation went something like this:

"Did you see people healed at the services?"

"Well, people were helped a lot, and some of them got better."

"I mean, did you ever see something that you would call a miracle, like the miracles in the New Testament? Something that could not be put down to medical help, remission, or recovery taking its natural course? Something that could not be put down to psychology? Something that was clearly a case of supernatural healing?"

It was at this point that my questions always seemed to get stuck. The only straight answers that I got were negative answers.

Changing moods

Back in the sixties, trendy theologians were grabbing the headlines with their talk about "the death of God." They ridiculed the idea of God coming to the rescue of people. If God existed at all (and many were doubtful), he certainly could not be expected to intervene in human affairs. The miracle stories of the Bible were relegated to the scrap heap of legend and myth, and the mood in many churches reflected the pessimism and negative outlook of the theologians and church leaders. But today the mood has changed. The trendy theologians of the past are themselves on the scrap heap. In many places it is not the believers in the supernatural who are treated as odd but those who raise questions.

Belief in the supernatural and miraculous is not confined to churchgoers. We cannot go through the check-out lines at the supermarket without seeing a half-dozen different magazines with lurid headlines designed to attract the casual purchaser. Students of such matters (like an anthropologist friend of mine) note two constant themes behind the headlines: the lives of the rich and famous, and the popular fascination with the bizarre and unusual. You do not have to be a genius to see that folklore and superstition are alive and well in the Western world today.

How does Christianity fit into this? The answer we get depends on whom we ask. Some simply dismiss belief in the miraculous as so much folklore. But others, though they may be doubtful about many of the stories they hear, do not want to dismiss miracles outright. Among Christians, two schools of thought have emerged. One says that the age of miracles is past. Miracles were given as divine attestation to the authority of Jesus and to the truth of the gospel. Once that proof was given, there was no need for it to be repeated.

But to the second school of thought this answer sounds almost like deism; as if God is no longer active in the world. Some members of this school go so far as to say that miracles are needed in the world today to convince people of the power of the gospel. Without "power encounters" that demonstrate the superior power of Christ, they believe the gospel would make no headway. But to members of the first school this seems to say that if miracles did not exist, it would be necessary to invent them. And to these observers, many of the present-day claims to miracles just do not ring true.

Which school is right? How should we go about making up our minds? There are two tests that we can apply: we can look at appeals to experience, and we can examine the teaching of Scripture. By applying both tests we can approach the question from opposite ends. We can look at the results that are claimed, and we can look at the Scriptures to which people turn in their expectation of miracles today.

Appeal to experience

There are two good reasons for taking a hard look at the appeal to experience. First, most claims to miracles today begin by appealing to experience. And second, whenever people claim that something is a fact, they are automatically inviting inspection of their claim. If we say that something is a fact, we have to be willing to show that there is a state of affairs that corresponds to the claim and that we are in a position to substantiate it.

This is a simple truth of everyday life. If an advertiser claims something for a product, the product must live up to the claim. This truth applies all the more if we claim to have experienced a miracle. In this case we have a moral obligation to meet two conditions. On the one hand, we must be able to show that the event did in fact occur. Otherwise, it is a nonevent. On the other hand, we must have grounds for believing that the event was in some way *miraculous*. Otherwise, we must face the question "What was there to distinguish the miracle from an *ordinary* nonmiraculous event?"

Unfortunately, many claims to miracles are open to criticism on both scores. Stories are published about answered prayer for healing, but the reader is rarely told of the relapses that followed. Testimonies are given to healings, but the role of medical treatment is often downplayed. When healing occurs, the charismatic healer receives the credit. When it fails to happen, the failure is attributed to other factors.

To say this is not to deny that God wonderfully answers prayer for healing today. Rather, it is to admit frankly that the church needs to do a better job of tracking and substantiating claims to miracles. We need to look squarely at the indictments in books such as William A. Nolen's *Healing: A Doctor in Search of a Miracle* (Random House, 1975) and James Randi's *The Faith Healers* (Prometheus Books, 1987). These are two very different books by two very different authors. Nolen was a surgeon whose investigation of healing claims ranged from psychic surgery to the ministry of Kathryn Kuhlman. Randi is a professional conjuror who unabashedly lays claim to possess "a narrow but rather strong expertise: I know what fakery looks like." Aided by a team of colleagues with similar expertise (sometimes disguised), Randi examined a number of contemporary healers, with devastating results.

To say that we need to face up to books such as these is not a sellout to skepticism. It is rather a call to self-examination. It is a call to recognize that when we claim miracles occur, we are putting God's reputation on the line. It is a challenge to listen to what a friend of mine said to me recently—a friend, incidentally, who is a keen member of a large church with a reputation for healing ministries—"Integrity can get lost in the middle of excitement."

It is not only skeptics outside the church who question the veracity of modern miracle stories. Seventy years ago the great evangelical scholar and champion of biblical inerrancy, B. B. Warfield, wrote a book entitled *Counterfeit Miracles*. Since then it has gone through several reprints and changes of title. (In the 1950s Eerdmans published it under the title *Miracles: Yesterday and Today, True and False*, and it is now back in print under its original title, published by the Banner of Truth, Carlisle, England.) Warfield wrote his book in the shadow of an illness that afflicted his wife from their honeymoon onward. Warfield did not deny that God answers prayer for healing. He believed that James 5:14 encourages such prayer. But he viewed the verse not as an encouragement to expect a miracle in the sense of God setting aside the normal processes of healing, but as an encouragement to ask God to work through the processes of the creation that he created. No book is perfect, and Warfield's is not without flaws. Nevertheless, it remains the most thorough examination of testimony to the miraculous from the early church down to Lourdes and Christian Science in Warfield's own day.

No other book written before or after Warfield embraces so wide a field with such rigor. A more recent study by an evangelical that examines miraculous claims associated with evangelical teachers is Henry Frost's *Miraculous Healing: A Personal Testimony and Biblical Study* (reprinted by Zondervan in 1979 with a foreword by Joni Eareckson). An examination of the evidence presented by Warfield and Frost suggests two conclusions. On the one hand, God has not ceased to answer prayer for healing, sometimes in extraordinary ways, but most often not apart from loving care and proper medical treatment. On the other hand, there is a sheer lack of solid evidence to support the claim that miracles of the kind found in the Bible have continued down the ages. There are not grounds in history for saying, "If only we had the faith, God would resume doing the miracles that he did in New Testament times."

The appeal to Scripture: Three mistakes

Does Scripture encourage us to expect miracles today like those depicted in the Gospels? In applying this second test we shall first note three common mistakes and then look at some passages that are often quoted by those who say we should expect biblical miracles today.

The first common mistake is to assume that certain passages of Scripture that have a specific application can be applied generally today. The classic case is Luke 4:18: "The Spirit of the Lord is upon me, because he has anointed me to preach good news to the poor. He has sent me to proclaim release to the captives and recovering of sight to the blind, to set at liberty those who are oppressed." These words were spoken by Jesus in the synagogue at Nazareth. He had entered the synagogue and was given the Book of the prophet Isaiah. He opened it at Isaiah 61:1, and after reading from it he declared, "Today this scripture has been fulfilled in your hearing" (Luke 4:21). This incident led to an attempt on his life. The point that needs to be stressed is that this prophecy applies to Jesus alone. It refers to his anointing by the Holy Spirit after his baptism. By reading from this Scripture and applying it to himself, Jesus was laying claim to be the Messiah. (The Hebrew word *Mashiach*, like its Greek translation *Christos*, means "anointed.") Jesus alone is the Christ, the Anointed One, and no one else may lay claim to this anointing and this role.

Other examples of texts that are often misapplied regarding miracles are found in the Epistles. When Paul spoke of "the signs of an apostle" (2 Cor. 12:12), he was talking strictly about the signs that God had wrought through *him* as an apostle. But the office of apostle ceased only with the first century. It was not an office that continued through the ages in the church, and we should not expect to see the "signs of an apostle" continued today. Another misapplied text is Hebrews 2:4, which says that God "bore witness by signs and wonders and various miracles and by gifts of the Holy Spirit distributed according to his own will." This refers to the ministry of Jesus and the founding of the church. The passage is not talking about what happens when the gospel is proclaimed in each and every age.

The second common mistake is to fail to distinguish between the different commands of Christ. Jesus instructed the Twelve to "heal the sick, raise the dead, cleanse lepers, cast out demons" (Matt. 10:8). But this was a special mission. Jesus went on to say: "You received without pay, give without pay. Take no gold, nor silver, nor copper in your belts, no bag for your journey, nor two tunics, nor sandals, nor a staff; for the laborer deserves his food" (10:9–10). It is funny how some people appeal to the first part of these instructions and claim that they apply today, but ignore the rest. Even a cursory glance at this passage, however, shows that the disciples' mission had limited goals. They were forbidden to go to the Gentiles and Samaritans and were charged with going to the "lost sheep of the house of Israel" (10:6).

When we turn to the Great Commission at the end of Matthew, we find no mention at all of miracles or healing. The commission of the risen Christ to go and make disciples of all nations, baptizing them in the name of the Father and of the Son and of the Holy Spirit, teaching them to observe all that Christ has commanded, makes no mention of miracles (Matt. 28:19–20). Nor, for that matter, does Luke's account. According to Luke, the disciples were instructed "that repentance and forgiveness of sins should be preached in his name to all nations, beginning from Jerusalem" (Luke 24:47). Similarly, John's account stresses forgiveness of sins (John 20:23). John mentions "signs," but the signs that he is concerned with are those that Jesus performed in his earthly life. It is these signs that are the ground for faith (John 20:30–31).

Someone may object that this leaves out Mark 16:9–20, which contains the promise that signs will accompany those who believe and the further promise that the disciples will be able to speak in new tongues, pick up snakes, drink deadly poison, and heal people by the laying on of hands. This passage is the so-called longer ending of Mark. Readers of modern translations of the Bible will see that this passage is only one of several endings of Mark that circulated in the early church. The RSV notes that "Some of the most ancient authorities bring the book to a close at the end of verse 8." My copy of the NIV prints the passage separately and inserts after Mark 16:8: "The most reliable early manuscripts and other ancient witnesses do not have Mark 16:9–20."

To my mind, the most likely explanation is that the Gospel of Mark ended at Mark 16:8. Someone, however, felt that more needed to be said, and an ending was constructed from material found in Acts (e.g., Acts 2:4–11, 37–42; 10:46; 19:6; 28:3–6). This material was presented as if it belonged to the commission of the risen Christ to the disciples. It is not found in the accounts of the commission in the other Gospels, as we have seen, nor is it to be found in the earliest manuscripts of Mark. We must therefore conclude that this passage was not originally part of Mark's Gospel or part of Christ's commission to the church. One further fact must be stressed. To say that Mark 16:9–20 is not part of Scripture is not a token of a low view of Scripture, but the reverse. It is because scholars such as Warfield and the translators of the NIV have the highest view of the authority of Scripture that they are concerned to distinguish between what is actual Scripture and what was added at a later date. It is because I share this view of the authority of Scripture and the words of Jesus that I believe it to be essential to separate them from later additions that have found their way into the text of certain manuscripts.

The third common mistake we need to recognize is the claim that salvation means wholeness here and now: If the kingdom has come, we should expect to see the blessings of the kingdom. Various arguments are put forward in support of this claim. It is sometimes said that there is healing in the Atonement. It is sometimes argued that the privileges of the believer under the New Covenant are greater than those under the old. It is also argued that God's concern is for our *shalom*, our peace. This is not only peace of mind or peace generally but also overall well-being, which includes health and prosperity. None of these arguments, however, adds up to a promise that we can expect a continued succession of miracles today.

Matthew 8:17 sees in the healings of Jesus a fulfillment of the prophecy of Isaiah 53:4: "This was to fulfill what was spoken by the prophet Isaiah, 'He took our infirmities and bore our diseases.' "But if we look closely at what Matthew is saying, it is clear that he is not talking about ongoing miracles or even about the atoning death of Christ. He is simply saying that Jesus' healing of the sick was a fulfillment of the part of Isaiah's servant prophecy that speaks of his identification of himself with our human condition. Even if we were to go on to say that the Atonement is the ground of our ultimate victory over all our ills and enemies, it would not follow that we experience the full fruits of it here and now.

It is true that the New Testament makes it clear that the privileges of the believer are greater under the New Covenant than they were under the Old Covenant. Christian greetings speak frequently of grace and peace (e.g., Rom. 1:7; 1 Cor. 1:3). Paul could assure his readers that "the peace of God, which passes all understanding, will keep your hearts and your minds in Christ Jesus" (Phil. 4:7). But this was a peace in the midst of such trials as imprisonment, impending death (Phil. 1:12–26), and illness (Phil. 2:25–27). These trials were overcome not by "miracles," in the sense of the supernatural suspension of normal processes, but by God's gracious ordering of events.

As a matter of fact, the Bible knows no single composite picture of wholeness consisting of health, wealth, and happiness as the birthright of every born-again Christian. The Beatitudes say nothing about material wealth, health, or ongoing miracles (Matt. 5:1–12; Luke 6:20–23), though they have much to say about hardships and the cost of discipleship. The Sermon on the Mount actually contains warnings against expectations of wholeness. It is better to lose the eye or hand that sins than that the whole body be thrown into hell (Matt. 5:29–30; 18:8–9; Mark 9:43–48).

Paul's "thorn in the flesh" (2 Cor. 12:7) is a further reminder that even an apostle who worked miracles (2 Cor. 12:12) could also suffer affliction. It is sometimes said that Paul is talking here about a "weakness" and not an illness, and that the "thorn in the flesh" was perhaps an opponent. All kinds of theories have been put forward about it, and perhaps we can never be certain exactly what it was. However, some things are certain. One of them is that the word translated as "weakness" (*astheneia*) also means "sickness" or "infirmity" in numerous places. It occurs in Matthew 8:17 in the passage quoted from Isaiah that we have just been looking at.

Other passages where *astheneia* has the meaning of "sickness," "infirmity," or "ailment" are Luke 5:15; 8:2; 13:11–12; John 5:5; 11:4; Acts 28:9; 1 Timothy 5:23; and Hebrews 11:34. Of particular interest is its use in Galatians 4:13, where Paul says: "You know it was because of a bodily ailment *[astheneia]* that I preached the gospel to you at first." Evidently his ailment compelled him to remain for a time in Galatia, where he took the opportunity to preach the gospel. The passage goes on, moreover, to suggest that the problem in question was something to do with Paul's eyesight. For he recalls that they would have plucked out their own eyes and given them to him, if it would have done any good (Gal. 4:15). But Paul was not living in the age of eye transplants.

The suggestion that Paul suffered from eye trouble is further supported by his reference to the large letters that he wrote with his own hand at the end of the letter to the Galatians (6:11). It also fits with his being temporarily blinded on the Damascus Road (Acts 9, 22, and 26), his apparent failure to recognize the high priest (Acts 23:2–5), and the fact that Paul's letters were regularly taken down by companions who served as secretaries (e.g., Rom. 16:22; 1 Cor. 1:1; 16:21; Col. 4:18). It is perhaps reinforced by the fact that Luke "the beloved physician" was one of Paul's companions in his later years (Col. 4:14). And ironically, it fits the context of 2 Corinthians 12 with its reference to visions, signs and wonders, and mighty works.

Although we may never know what exactly was Paul's "thorn in the flesh," we do know that it did not go away. Paul made it a matter of persistent prayer. He received God's answer. God did not remove the "thorn in the flesh" but told him, "My grace is sufficient for you, for my power is made perfect in weakness" (2 Cor. 12:9).

The promises of God
The sufficiency of God's grace is a central theme of Scripture. Failure to recognize this lies at the root of so many false expectations, misguided actions, spiritual depressions, and disillusionments. This failure is really a failure to appreciate and accept what God has promised. The God of the Bible is a promise-keeping God. The promise of God has a common theme: "I will be your God, and

you shall be my people." It is a theme that unites the Old and New Testaments (Lev. 26:12; 2 Cor. 6:15–18). But does this mean that we can expect miracles to happen all the time?

If we turn to the Old Testament, the answer to this question is clearly no. We do not find miracle stories evenly distributed throughout the Old Testament. They occur at special times of redemptive history, like the time of the Exodus (Exod. 8–17) and the time of Elijah and Elisha (1 Kings 17–18; 2 Kings 2–7). For long periods of history, miracles are not mentioned. But what about those passages in the New Testament that people quote in the expectation of miracles today? Let us look at three of them: the promise concerning greater works, the saying that faith moves mountains, and the teaching in James about prayer for the sick.

John 14:12–14 contains the promise of Jesus: "He who believes in me will also do the works that I do; and greater works than these will he do, because I go to the Father. . . . If you ask anything in my name, I will do it." Does this mean that we should all expect to perform miracles? Like so many other statements in the fourth Gospel, this statement has a cryptic quality about it. On the one hand, in the literal, physical sense the disciples did not do greater works. The disciples did not change water into wine, feed 5,000 people from a small quantity of loaves and fish, or walk on water. Although they did astonishing things, not even the raising of Dorcas (Acts 9:36–43) was as striking as the raising of Lazarus who had been in the tomb four days (John 11:39).

On the other hand, the ministry of the apostles extended beyond the geographic limits of Jesus' ministry. They won more people to faith. But perhaps the best clues to the meaning of the passage are provided by the other verses about the "work of God" in this Gospel. John 5:20 speaks of "greater works," which are explained as the Son giving life to the dead and granting eternal life to those who believe. The "work of God" is described in John 6:28–29 as believing in him whom God has sent. If we follow the thought of John 14:12 as it is worked out in the rest of the Gospel, we see that the disciples are given the promise and the charge to bear fruit (John 15:16), which again is linked with the invitation to ask the Father in Jesus' name. The disciples are promised the Paraclete, who will convict the world of sin, righteousness, and judgment (John 16:7–11). And finally, in

John 20:22–23 they are given the Holy Spirit, with the authority to forgive and retain sins.

In other words, there is nothing in John 14 or in the rest of John to suggest that the "greater works" are greater physical miracles. Physical miracles are in fact lesser works compared with those that have to do with the conviction of sin, forgiveness, judgment, salvation, and eternal life.

The same must be said about the promise concerning the mountain being cast into the midst of the sea (Matt. 21:20–22; Mark 11:20–24). People often talk about faith moving mountains. Jesus was not talking about mountains in general, however, but about "this mountain." The saying was prompted by the disciples' wonder at the withering of the fig tree that Jesus had cursed. There is clearly no thought in the passage about miracles of healing. If anything, there is a pronouncement of judgment. The imagery weaves together a number of Old Testament themes—the mountain of the Lord (Isa. 2; Mic. 4), the setting of God's king on Zion, his holy hill (Ps. 2:6), the mountains shaking in the midst of the sea (Ps. 46:2). If "this mountain" refers to Mount Zion, the saying is a word of encouragement to the disciples in turbulent times. The old order, centered on Jerusalem as the mountain of the Lord, had rejected Jesus. It had failed to bear fruit in response to the coming of Jesus, and it was about to destroy him and threaten the lives of his followers. But the disciples are given a word of encouragement that this seemingly insufferable threat will be overcome. In view of the following saying about forgiveness, the saying may also recall Micah 7:19: "Thou wilt cast all our sins into the depths of the sea."

But what about James 5:13–16? The sick are instructed to summon the elders of the church to pray over them and anoint them with oil in the name of the Lord. The assurance is given that "the prayer of faith will save the sick man, and the Lord will raise him up." Two things are clear from this passage. One is that James is not talking about miracles as such. If he is talking about healing at all, he is talking about prayer for healing in general. The other is the fact that James is not speaking about evangelistic healing services to which anybody may come. The situation is not comparable to those healing stories in which all and sundry came to Jesus for healing. James is talking about sick people *within* the church and what the elders should do for church members who are sick. Even so, the promise cannot be regarded as absolute. For sooner or later everyone has to die.

In view of this, it is possible that James is not talking about the healing of the sick, but about ministry to the dying. This was the view that was widely held in the early church. Evidently the person that James is discussing is too sick to attend the meetings of the church. The elders have to come to him. Moreover, a note of ambiguity may be heard in James's language. The words *save* and *raise up* can be used to refer to healing and to raising from the sickbed. But they are also used to refer to healing from sin and death and to resurrection to eternal life. The word *heal* can mean restoration to health. But it can also mean healing from sin. Perhaps the passage is best understood as a word of encouragement to those who face death.

The suggestion that James has in mind a ministry of the church to the dying fits the general argument of his letter. Earlier James has denounced the dead faith that produces no works. But what if a person is dying and is unable to do any good works? It may be that James's statement that the prayer of faith will save the sick and that the Lord will raise him up, is an assurance that those who are reconciled to God and the church will be raised in the resurrection and have their sins forgiven.

Simple solutions

I think it was H. L. Mencken who observed that for every complex problem there is always a simple solution—which is almost invariably wrong. The same can be said about miracles and healing. The simplistic solutions of the extremists on both sides are attractive precisely because they are simple. But it is as wrong to say that the church has no part at all in the ministry of healing as it is to say that the only thing that prevents people from being healed today is their lack of faith in miracles.

A hard look at the evidence does not support the claim that miracles like those described in the Gospels are continually happening today. Nor does Scripture encourage us to expect that miracles will be part of everyday life. If they were—as Augustine observed long ago—people would take them for granted, just as they do the daily miracles of nature.

But to say this is not the same as saying that gifts of healing have totally disappeared (1 Cor. 12:9–10; Gal. 3:5). There are those who have special ministries of prayer and healing of the sick in body and spirit. Such ministries today, however, are ministries that work *in conjunction with* the medical and healing professions. In the case of Jesus, his miracles were performed *independently* of those professions. Moreover, the "miracles" that people talk about today are primarily miracles of healing. They do not include nature miracles, like those of Jesus.

The most inclusive definition of a miracle is to describe it as God's interference with the course of nature. Interference with the course of nature can take various forms. As C. S. Lewis pointed out, human beings interfere with the course of nature all the time. When I close a window, I am interfering with the air that is blowing in. Such interference does not involve suspension of the laws of nature. Rather, it determines what factors will come into play. In our normal relationship with God, God does not suspend the laws of nature. As a personal being, he interferes with the course of events in ways similar to those in which we as personal beings interfere with the course of events. If God did not act, events would take a different course. When we pray, we do so in the expectation that God can and does act in human affairs. But not every act of God is a miracle in the narrower sense of the term. Not every action of God is a miracle in the sense that the resurrection of Jesus was a miracle. The reason for this lies in the distinction between what C. S. Lewis has called "miracles of the old creation" and "miracles of the new creation." In a "miracle of the old creation," God, drawing on the resources that are already present in nature, interferes with the present order of things. In a "miracle of the new creation," the reality of the new order of the world to come breaks into our present reality. In the case of the resurrection of Jesus, his resurrection body, which belongs to the new order of the world to come, entered our order of space and time.

For this reason it is not surprising that such miracles do not occur in our everyday experience. The resurrection of Jesus gives us a glimpse into the world to come. But it is not part of our present reality. It is a mistake, therefore, to expect realities that belong to the world to come to happen in the here and now. Scripture encourages us to live by the promise of God. God has given his covenanted promise that those who turn to him for forgiveness of their sins will have their sins forgiven. But we do not have a similar, parallel promise of miracles here and now. We can say to everyone that God will forgive them if they truly turn to him. But we cannot say to them that God will perform a miracle for them, if only they believe. This does not mean that God cannot work miracles today or that he has not worked miracles since the days of the New Testament. But it does mean that we need to recognize the difference between God's covenanted mercies and God's uncovenanted mercies.

Chapter 6

SHOULD CHRISTIANS SEEK THE GIFT OF PROPHECY STILL TODAY?

Wayne A. Grudem

One key difference between many evangelicals and charismatic believers is their attitude toward the gift of prophecy. In charismatic worship, it is not unusual for one or more persons to deliver "a word from the Lord." Some evangelicals believe Scripture has ruled out that possibility. Others feel uneasy or just plain skeptical when face to face with someone who claims to speak on God's behalf.

In this essay, exegete Wayne Grudem examines what the New Testament says about the gift of prophecy, suggests a new definition for this gift, and offers biblical counsel for its use in both charismatic and noncharismatic churches.

Can evangelical Christians use the gift of prophecy in their churches today? What is this spiritual gift, and how does it function? If we do allow for its use, how can we guard against its abuse and preserve the unique authority of Scripture in our lives?

The New Testament teaches that the gift of prophecy should be defined not as "predicting the future," nor as "proclaiming a word from the Lord," nor as "powerful preaching," but rather as "telling something that God has spontaneously brought to mind." Once we understand prophecy in this way, we can allow our churches room to enjoy one of the Holy Spirit's most edifying gifts.

Less authority than Scripture

How was the gift of prophecy viewed by the New Testament church? We may begin our investigation of this gift by comparing its authority with that of the Old Testament prophets and the apostles in the early church. Old Testament prophets had an amazing responsibility—they were able to speak and write words that had absolute divine authority. They could say, "Thus says the Lord," and the words that followed were the very words of God. The prophets wrote their words as God's words in Scripture for all time (see Deut. 18:18–20; Num. 22:38; Jer. 1:9; Ezek. 2:7). To disbelieve or disobey a prophet's words, therefore, was to disbelieve or disobey God (Deut. 18:19; 1 Sam. 8:7; 1 Kings 20:36).

In the New Testament we also find people who could speak and write God's very words and have them recorded in Scripture, but we are surprised to find that Jesus no longer calls them "prophets." He uses a new term, "apostles." The apostles are the New Testament counterpart to the Old Testament prophets (see 1 Cor. 2:13; 14:37; 2 Cor. 13:3; Gal. 1:8–9, 11–12; 2 Thess. 2:13; 4:8, 15; 2 Peter 3:2). It is the apostles, not the prophets, who have authority to write the words of New Testament Scripture. When the apostles want to establish their unique authority, they never appeal to the title *prophet;* they call themselves *apostles* (Rom. 1:1; 1 Cor. 1:1; 9:1–2; 2 Cor. 1:1; 11:12–13; 12:11–12; Gal. 1:1; Eph. 1:1; 1 Peter 1:1; 2 Peter 1:1; 3:2).

The word *prophet* in New Testament times

Why did Jesus choose the new term *apostle* to designate those who had the authority to write Scripture? It was probably because at the time of the New Testament, the Greek word *prophētēs* ("prophet") had a very broad range of meanings. It generally did not have the sense of "one who speaks God's very words," but rather indicated "one who speaks on the basis of some external influence" (often a spiritual influence of some kind). Titus 1:12 uses the word in this sense when Paul quotes Epimenides, a pagan Greek poet: "One of themselves, a prophet of their own, said 'Cretans are always liars, evil beasts, lazy gluttons.' " The soldiers who mock Jesus also seem to use the word *prophesy* in this way, when they blindfold Jesus and cruelly demand, "Prophesy! Who is it that struck you?" (Luke 22:64). They don't mean "Speak words of absolute divine authority," but "Tell us something that has been revealed to you" (also cf. John 4:19).

Many writings outside the Bible use the Greek word *prophētēs* in this way without signifying any divine authority in the words of the one so labeled. In fact, by the time of the New Testament the term *prophet* in everyday use often just meant "one who has supernatural knowledge" or "one who predicts the future"—or even simply "spokesman," without any connotation of divine authority.

Several examples near the time of the New Testament are given in Helmut Krämer's article in the *Theological Dictionary of the New Testament* (Eerdmans, 1969, vol. 6, p. 794):

A philosopher is called "a prophet of immortal nature" (Dio Chrysostom, A.D. 40–120).

A teacher (Diogenes) wants to be "a prophet of truth and candor" (Lucian of Samosata, A.D. 120–180).

Those who advocate Epicurean philosophy are called "prophets of Epicurus" (Plutarch, A.D. 50–120).

Written history is called "the prophetess of truth" (Diodorus Siculus, who wrote ca. 60–30 B.C.).

A "specialist" in botany is called a "prophet" (Dioscurides of Cilicia, first century A.D.).

A "quack" in medicine is called a "prophet" (Galen of Pergamum, A.D. 129–99).

Krämer concludes that the Greek word for *prophet* "simply expresses the formal function of declaring, proclaiming, making known." Yet because "every prophet declares something which is not his own," the Greek word for *herald (kērux)* "is the closest synonym" (p. 795).

The words *prophet* and *prophecy* could, of course, sometimes be used of the apostles when the context was emphasizing an external spiritual influence (from the Holy Spirit) under which they spoke (see Eph. 2:20; 3:5; Rev. 1:3; 22:7), but this was not the ordinary terminology used for the apostles, and the terms *prophet* and *prophecy* did not in themselves imply divine authority for their speech or writing.

Much more commonly, these words were used of ordinary Christians who spoke *not* with absolute divine authority but simply to report something God had laid on their hearts or brought to their minds. There are many indications in the New Testament that this ordinary gift of prophecy had less authority than that of the Bible, and even less than that of recognized Bible teaching in the early church.

Prophecy must be based on a spontaneous "revelation"
If prophecy does not contain God's very words, then what is it? In what sense is it from God?

Paul indicates that God could bring something spontaneously to mind so that the person prophesying would report it in his or her own words. Paul calls this a "revelation": "If a revelation is made to another sitting by, let the first be silent. For you can all prophesy one by one, so that all may learn and all be encouraged" (1 Cor. 14:30–31). Here he uses the word *revelation* in a broader sense than the technical way theologians have used it to speak of words equal to Scripture in authority. The terms *reveal* and *revelation* are also used elsewhere in the New Testament in this broader sense of communication from God that does not result in written Scripture or in words equal to written Scripture in authority (see Matt. 11:27; Rom. 1:18; Eph. 1:17; Phil. 3:15).

Paul is simply referring to something God may suddenly bring to mind or something God may impress on someone's heart or thoughts in such a way that the person has a sense that it is from God. The thought brought to mind may be surprisingly distinct from the person's own train of thought, or it may be accompanied by some sense of urgency or persistence, or in some other way it may give the person a rather clear sense that it is from the Lord.

Thus, if a stranger comes in and all prophesy, "the secrets of his heart are disclosed; and so, falling on his face, he will worship God and declare that God is really among you" (1 Cor. 14:25). I have heard a report of this happening in a noncharismatic Baptist church in America. A missionary speaker paused in the middle of his message and said something like this: "I didn't plan to say this, but it seems the Lord is indicating that someone in this church has just walked out on his wife and family. If that is so, let me tell you that God wants you to return to them and learn to follow God's pattern for family life." The missionary did not know it, but in the unlit balcony sat a man who had entered the church moments before for the first time in his life. The description fit him exactly, and he made himself known, acknowledged his sin, and began to seek after God.

In this way, prophecy serves as a "sign" for believers (1 Cor. 14:22)—it is a clear demonstration that God is definitely at work in their midst, a "sign" of God's hand of blessing on the congregation. And since it will work for the conversion of unbelievers as well, Paul encourages the use of this gift when "unbelievers or outsiders enter" (1 Cor. 14:23–24).

Many of us have experienced or heard of similar events. For example, an unplanned but urgent request may be given to pray for certain missionaries in Nigeria. Much later those who prayed discover that just at that time the missionaries had been in an auto accident or at a point of intense spiritual conflict and had needed those prayers. Paul would call the sense or intuition of those things a "revelation," and the report to the assembled church of that prompting from God, a "prophecy." It may have elements of the speaker's own understanding or interpretation in it, and it certainly needs evaluation and testing, yet it has a valuable function in the church.

New Testament examples of lesser authority
In Acts 21:4 we read of the disciples at Tyre: "Through the Spirit they told Paul not to go on to Jerusalem." This seems to be a reference to prophecy directed toward Paul, but Paul disobeyed it! He never would have done this if this prophecy contained God's very words.

In Acts 21:10–11, Agabus prophesied that the Jews at Jerusalem would "bind [Paul] and deliver him into the hands of the Gentiles," a prediction that was nearly correct but not quite: The Romans were the ones who bound Paul (v. 33), and the Jews, rather than delivering him voluntarily, tried to kill him, and he had to be rescued by force (v. 32). The prediction was not far off, but it contained inaccuracy in detail that would have called into question the validity of any Old Testament prophet.

Paul tells the Thessalonians: "Do not despise prophesying, but test everything; hold fast what is good" (1 Thess. 5:20–21). If prophecy had equaled God's word in authority, he would never have had to tell the Thessalonians not to despise it—they "received" and "accepted" God's word "with joy inspired by the Holy Spirit" (1 Thess. 1:6; 2:13; cf. 4:15). But when Paul tells them to "test everything," he must be including at least the prophecies he mentioned in the previous phrase. He implies that prophecies contain some things that are good and some things that are not good when he encourages them to "hold fast what is good." This is something that could never have been said of the words of an Old Testament prophet or of the authoritative teachings of a New Testament apostle.

In Acts 21:9, moreover, we read that Philip had "four unmarried daughters, who prophesied." Whatever we may think about the appropriateness of women teaching the Bible today, this prophesying by Philip's daughters would be difficult to reconcile with New Testament prohibitions against authoritative teaching by women (see 1 Tim. 2:12) if prophecy had absolute divine authority or even if it had authority greater than or equal to Bible teaching. Similar reasoning applies to 1 Corinthians 11:5, where Paul allows women to prophesy in church, even though he later apparently forbids them to speak up publicly during the evaluation or judging of prophecies (1 Cor. 14:34–35).

More extensive evidence on New Testament prophecy is found in 1 Corinthians 14. When Paul says, "Let two or three prophets speak and let the others weigh what is said" (1 Cor. 14:29), he suggests that they should listen carefully and sift the good from the bad, accepting some and rejecting the rest (this is the implication of the Greek word *diakrinō*, here translated "weigh what is said"). We cannot imagine an Old Testament prophet such as Isaiah saying, "Listen to what I say and weigh what is said—sort the good from the bad—sift what you accept from what you should not accept!" If prophecy had absolute divine authority, it would be sin to do this. But here Paul commands that it be done, which suggests that New Testament prophecy did not have the authority of God's very words.

In 1 Corinthians 14:30–31, Paul allows one prophet to interrupt another one: "If a revelation is made to another sitting by, let the first be silent. For you can all prophesy one by one." Again, if prophets were speaking God's very words, equal in value to Scripture, it is hard to imagine that Paul would say they should be interrupted and not allowed to finish their message. But this is what Paul commands.

Paul suggests that no one at Corinth, a church that experienced a great deal of prophecy, was able to speak God's very words. He says in 1 Corinthians 14:36, "What! Did the word of God come forth from you, or are you the only ones it has reached?"

Then in verses 37 and 38, he claims authority far greater than any prophet at Corinth: "If anyone thinks that he is a prophet, or spiritual, he should acknowledge that what I am writing to you is a command of the Lord. If anyone does not recognize this, he is not recognized."

All these passages indicate that the common idea that in the early church prophets spoke "words of the Lord" when the apostles were not present is simply incorrect.

In addition to the verses we have considered so far, there is one other type of evidence that suggests that New Testament congregational prophets spoke with less authority than New Testament apostles or Scripture. It concerns the problem of successors to the apostles. We find that it is solved not by encouraging Christians to listen to the prophets but by pointing to the Scriptures.

Paul, at the end of his life, emphasizes "rightly handling the word of truth" (2 Tim. 2:15), and the "God-breathed" character of Scripture "for teaching, for reproof, for correction, and for training in righteousness" (2 Tim. 3:16). Jude urges his readers to "contend for the faith which was once for all delivered to the saints" (Jude 3). Peter, at the end of his life, encourages his readers to "pay attention" to Scripture, which is like "a lamp shining in a dark place" (2 Peter 1:19–20), and reminds them of the teaching of the apostle Paul "in all his letters" (2 Peter 3:16).

In no case do we read exhortations to "give heed to the prophets in your churches" or to "obey the words of the Lord through your prophets." Yet there certainly were prophets prophesying in many local congregations after the death of the apostles. It seems that they did not have authority equal to the apostles and that the authors of Scripture knew this.

Prophecy as merely human words

We may conclude that prophecies are not "the words of God" today. Prophecies in the church should be considered merely human words, *not* God's words, and not equal to God's words in authority. But does this conclusion conflict with current charismatic teaching or practice? I think it conflicts with much charismatic *practice*, but not with most charismatic *teaching*.

Most charismatic teachers today would agree that contemporary prophecy is not equal to Scripture in authority. Though some will speak of prophecy as being the "word of God" for today, there is almost uniform testimony from all sections of the charismatic movement that prophecy is imperfect and impure, and will contain elements that are not to be obeyed or trusted. For example, Bruce Yocum, author of a widely used charismatic book on prophecy, writes: "Prophecy can be impure—our own thoughts or ideas can get mixed into the message we receive—whether we receive the words directly or only receive a sense of the message . . . (Paul says that all our prophecy is imperfect)" (*Prophecy*, Servant Publications, 1976, p. 79).

But it must be said that in actual practice a great deal of confusion results from the habit of prefacing prophecies with the common Old Testament phrase, "Thus says the Lord" (a phrase not used by any recorded prophets in New Testament churches). This is unfortunate, because it gives the impression that the words that follow are God's very words. The New Testament does not justify that position and, when pressed, most responsible charismatic spokesmen would not want to claim it for every part of their prophecies. There would be much gain and no loss if that introductory phrase were dropped.

It is true that Agabus uses a similar phrase ("Thus says the Holy Spirit") in Acts 21:11, but the same words (Greek: *tade legei*) are used by Christian writers just after the time of the New Testament to introduce very general paraphrases or greatly expanded interpretations of what is being reported (e.g., Ignatius, *Epistle to the Philadel-*

phians 7:1–2 [ca. A.D. 108] and *Epistle of Barnabas* 6:8; 9:2, 5 [A.D. 70–100]). The phrase can apparently mean "This is generally (or approximately) what the Holy Spirit is saying to us."

If someone really does think God is bringing something to mind that should be reported in the congregation, there is nothing wrong with saying, "I think the Lord is putting on my mind that . . ." or some similar expression. Of course, this does not sound as forceful as "Thus says the Lord," but if the message is really from God, the Holy Spirit will cause it to speak with great power to the hearts of those who need to hear.

The difference between prophecy and teaching

As far as we can tell, all New Testament "prophecy" was based on this kind of spontaneous prompting from the Holy Spirit (cf. Acts 11:28; 21:4, 10–11; and note the ideas of prophecy represented in Luke 7:39; 22:63–64; John 4:19; 11:51). Unless a person receives a spontaneous "revelation" from God, there is no prophecy.

In contrast, no human act of speech that is called a "teaching," that is done by a "teacher," or that is described by the verb "to teach" is ever in the New Testament said to be based on a "revelation." Rather, "teaching" is often simply an explanation or application of Scripture (Acts 15:35; 18:11, 25; Rom. 2:21; 15:4; Col. 3:16; Heb. 5:12) or a repetition and explanation of apostolic instructions (e.g., Rom. 16:17; 2 Tim. 2:2; 3:10). It is what we would call "Bible teaching" or "preaching" today.

Prophecy thus has less authority than teaching, and prophecies in the church are always to be subject to the authoritative teaching of Scripture. Timothy was not to prophesy Paul's instructions in the church; he was to teach them (1 Tim. 4:11; 6:2). Paul did not prophesy his ways in every church; he taught them (1 Cor. 4:17). The Thessalonians were not told to hold firm to the traditions that were "prophesied" to them but to the traditions that they were "taught" by Paul (2 Thess. 2:15). Contrary to some views, it was the teachers and not the prophets who gave leadership and direction to the early churches.

Among the elders, therefore, were "those who labor in preaching and *teaching*" (1 Tim. 5:17), and an elder was to be "an apt teacher" (1 Tim. 3:2; cf. Titus 1:9)—but nothing was said about any elders whose work was prophesying, nor was it ever said that an elder was to be "an apt prophet" or that elders should be "holding firm to sound prophecies." In his leadership function, Timothy was to take heed to himself and to his "teaching" (1 Tim. 4:16), but he was never told to take heed to his prophesying. James warned that those who *teach*, not those who prophesy, will be judged with greater strictness (James 3:1). The task of interpreting and applying Scripture, then, is called "teaching" in the New Testament. Although a few people have claimed that the prophets in New Testament churches gave "charismatically inspired" interpretations of Old Testament Scripture, that claim has not been persuasive, primarily because it is difficult to find any convincing examples in the New Testament where the "prophet" word group is used to refer to someone doing this kind of activity.

The distinction is quite clear: If a message is the result of conscious reflection on the text of Scripture, containing interpretation of the text and application to life, then it is (in New Testament terms) a *teaching*. But if a message is the report of something God brings suddenly to mind, then it is a *prophecy*. And, of course, even prepared teachings can be interrupted by unplanned additional material that the Bible teacher suddenly feels God is bringing to his mind—in that case, it would be a teaching with some prophecy mixed in.

The issue of subjectivity

At this point someone may object that waiting for such "promptings" from God is "too subjective" a process. My reply is that the people who make this objection are exactly the ones who need this subjective process most in their own Christian lives! This gift requires waiting on the Lord, listening for him, hearing his prompting in our hearts. For Christians who are completely evangelical, doctrinally sound, intellectual, and "objective," probably what is needed most is the strong, balancing influence of a more vital, "subjective" relationship with the Lord in everyday life. And these people are also those who have the *least* likelihood of being led into error, for they already place great emphasis on solid grounding in the Word of God.

Yet there is an opposite danger of excessive reliance on subjective impressions for guidance, and that must be clearly guarded against. People who continually seek subjective "messages" from God to guide their lives must be cautioned that subjective personal guidance is *not* a primary function of New Testament prophecy. They need to place much more emphasis on Scripture and seeking God's sure wisdom written there.

Many charismatic writers would agree with this caution, as the following examples indicate:

Michael Harper (Anglican charismatic pastor): "Prophecies which tell other people what they are to do—are to be regarded with great suspicion" (*Prophecy: A Gift for the Body of Christ*, Logos, 1964, p. 26).

Donald Gee (Assemblies of God): "Many of our errors where spiritual gifts are concerned arise when we want the extraordinary and exceptional to be made the frequent and habitual. Let all who develop excessive desire for 'messages' through the gifts take warning from the wreckage of past generations as well as of contemporaries. . . . The Holy Scriptures are a lamp unto our feet and a light unto our path" (*Spiritual Gifts in the Work of Ministry Today*, Gospel Publishing House, 1963, pp. 51–52).

Donald Bridge (British charismatic pastor): "The illuminist constantly finds that 'God tells him' to do things. . . . Illuminists are often very sincere, very dedicated, and possessed of a commitment to obey God that shames more cautious Christians. Nevertheless they are treading a dangerous path. Their ancestors have trodden it before, and always with disastrous results in the long run. Inner feelings and special promptings are by their very nature subjective. The Bible provides our objective guide" (*Signs and Wonders Today*, IVP-UK, 1985, p. 183).

What can prophecies say?

The examples of prophecies in the New Testament mentioned above show that the idea of prophecy as merely "predicting the future" is certainly wrong for the New Testament. It mentions some predictions (Acts 11:28; 21:11), but it also refers to the disclosure of sins (1 Cor. 14:25). In fact, *anything* that edified could have been included, for Paul says, "He who prophesies speaks to men for their upbuilding and encouragement and consolation" (1 Cor. 14:3). Here is another indication of the value of prophecy: It can speak to the needs of people's hearts in a spontaneous, direct way.

At two significant points in our marriage, my wife, Margaret, and I visited and prayed with Christian friends in another part of the United States. On both occasions during our time of prayer together, the husband of the family we were visiting paused and gently spoke just a sentence directly to Margaret. Each sentence touched her heart and brought the Lord's comfort regarding deep concerns that we had not mentioned at all to the other couple. Here is the value of prophecy for "upbuilding and encouragement and consolation" (1 Cor. 14:3).

Any Christian can prophesy

Another great benefit of prophecy is that it provides an opportunity for participation by everyone in the congregation, not just those who are skilled speakers or who have gifts of teaching. Paul says that he wants "all" the Corinthians to prophesy (1 Cor. 14:5), and he says, "You can all prophesy one by one, so that all may learn and all be encouraged" (1 Cor. 14:31). Greater openness to the gift of prophecy could help overcome the situation that exists when many who attend our churches are merely spectators and not participants. Perhaps we are contributing to the problem of "spectator Christianity" by quenching the work of the Spirit in this area.

The continuation of prophecy

Paul says, "Our prophecy is imperfect; but when the perfect comes, the imperfect will pass away" (1 Cor. 13:9–10). He thus tells us that prophecy will pass away at a certain time, namely, "when the perfect comes." But when is that? It has to be the time when the Lord returns. This is because it must be the same time that is indicated by the word "then" in verse 12: "Now we see in a mirror dimly, but *then* face to face. Now I know in part; *then* I shall understand fully, even as I have been fully understood."

To see "face to face" is an Old Testament phrase for seeing God personally (see Gen. 32:30; Exod. 33:11; Deut. 34:10; Judg. 6:22; Ezek. 20:35—these are the only Old Testament occurrences of this Greek phrase or its Hebrew equivalent, and they all refer to seeing God). The time when I shall understand "as I have been understood" also must refer to the Lord's return.

Some have argued that "when the perfect comes" refers to the time when the New Testament canon is complete. (Revelation, the last New Testament book written, was completed in A.D. 90 at the latest, about 35 years after Paul wrote 1 Corinthians.) But would the Corinthians ever have understood that from what Paul wrote? Is there any mention at all of a collection of New Testament books or a New Testament canon anywhere in the context of 1 Corinthians 13? Such an idea is foreign to the context. Moreover, such a statement would not fit Paul's purpose in the argument. Would it be persuasive to argue: "We can be sure that love will never end, for we know that it will last more than 35 years"? This would hardly be convincing. The context requires rather that Paul be contrasting this age with the age to come and saying that love will endure into eternity.

D. Martyn Lloyd-Jones observes that the view that makes "when the perfect comes" equal the time of the completion of the New Testament encounters another difficulty: "It means that you and I, who have the Scriptures open before us, know much more than the apostle Paul of God's truth.... It means that we are altogether superior ... even to the apostles themselves, including the apostle Paul! It means that we are now in a position in which ... 'we know, even as also we are known' by God.... indeed, there is only one word to describe such a view, it is nonsense" (*Prove All Things*, ed. Christopher Catherwood, Kingsway, 1985, pp. 32–33).

John Calvin, referring to 1 Corinthians 13:8–13, says, "It is stupid of people to make the whole of this discussion apply to the intervening time" (*The First Epistle of Paul the Apostle to the Corinthians*, trans. J. W. Fraser, ed. D. W. Torrance and T. F. Torrance, Eerdmans, 1960, p. 281).

This means we have a clear biblical statement that Paul expected the gift of prophecy to continue through the entire church age and to function for the benefit of the church until the Lord returns. Should we not be using it in our churches today?

Paul valued this gift so highly that he told the Corinthians, "Make love your aim, and earnestly desire the spiritual gifts, especially that you may prophesy" (1 Cor. 14:1). A little later he said, "He who prophesies edifies the church" (1 Cor. 14:4). Then, at the end of his discussion of spiritual gifts, he said again, "So, my brethren, earnestly desire to prophesy" (1 Cor. 14:39). If Paul was eager for the gift of prophecy to function at Corinth, troubled as that church was by immaturity, selfishness, divisions, and other problems, should we not also actively seek this valuable gift in our congregations today? If we are evangelicals who profess to believe and obey *all* that Scripture says, should we not also believe and obey this? And might a greater openness to the gift of prophecy perhaps help to correct a dangerous imbalance in our church lives, an imbalance that is too exclusively intellectual, objective, and narrowly doctrinal?

Encouraging and regulating prophecy
What if we decide that the gift of prophecy is something that should be encouraged in our own churches? What should we do?

For all Christians, and especially for pastors and others who have teaching responsibilities in the church, several steps would be both appropriate and pastorally wise:

1. Pray seriously for the Lord's wisdom on how and when to approach this subject in the church.

2. Teach on this subject, if you have teaching responsibilities, in the regular Bible teaching times that the church already provides.

3. Be patient and proceed slowly—church leaders should not be "domineering" (or "pushy"; 1 Peter 5:3), and a patient approach will avoid frightening people away or alienating them unnecessarily.

4. Recognize and encourage the gift of prophecy in the ways it has already been functioning in the church—at church prayer meetings, for example, when someone has felt unusually "led" by the Holy Spirit to pray for something, or when it has seemed that the Holy Spirit was bringing to mind a hymn or Scripture passage or giving a common sense of the tone or focus of a time of group worship or prayer. Even Christians in churches not open to the gift of prophecy can at least be sensitive to promptings from the Holy Spirit regarding what to pray for in church prayer meetings, and can then express those promptings in the form of a prayer (what might be called a "prophetic prayer") to the Lord.

5. If the first four steps have been followed, and *if the congregation and its leadership will accept it*, some opportunities for the use of the gift of prophecy might be made in the less-formal worship services of the church, such as Sunday evenings, Wednesday prayer meetings, or smaller house groups. If this is allowed, those who prophesy

should be kept within scriptural guidelines (1 Cor. 14:29–36), should genuinely seek the edification of the church and not their own prestige (1 Cor. 14:12, 26), and should not dominate the meeting or be overly dramatic or emotional in their speech (and thus attract attention to themselves rather than to the Lord). Prophecies should certainly be evaluated according to the teachings of Scripture (1 Cor. 14:29–36; 1 Thess. 5:19–21).

6. If the gift of prophecy begins to be used in your church, place even more emphasis on the vastly superior value of Scripture as the place where Christians can always go to hear the voice of the living God. Prophecy is a valuable gift, as are many other gifts, but it is in Scripture that God and only God speaks to us his very words, even today, and all through our lives. Rather than hope that the highlight at every worship service will be some word of prophecy, those who use this gift need to be reminded that we should direct our expectation of hearing from God toward the Bible, and that we should delight in God himself as he speaks to us through the Bible. There we have a treasure of infinite worth: the actual words of our Creator speaking to us in language we can understand. And rather than seeking frequent guidance through prophecy, we should emphasize that it is in Scripture that we are to find guidance for our lives. In Scripture is our source of direction, our focus when seeking God's will, our sufficient and completely reliable standard. It is of God's words in Scripture that we can say with confidence, "Thy word is a lamp to my feet and a light to my path" (Ps. 119:105).

What do we lose if we neglect prophecy?
Is this whole discussion really important? Will we lose anything if we go on as many of us have before, largely neglecting the gift of prophecy in our churches?

I believe much will be lost. First, if the argument presented here is correct, to neglect prophecy is to be disobedient to Scripture. That is reason enough to know that there will be negative consequences in our churches, and at least the lack of the full blessing that would be ours if we obeyed.

Second, without this gift of prophecy we will probably lose an element of closeness to God and sensitivity to his promptings in our daily walk.

Third, we will miss out on a measure of vitality in worship, the sense of awe that comes from seeing God at work at this very moment—the overwhelming sense of wonder that causes us to exclaim,"Truly God is in this place."

Chapter 7

SHOULD WOMEN BE ORDAINED TO CHRISTIAN MINISTRY?

Robert G. Clouse and Bonnidell A. Clouse

No question in the church seems to raise tempers more than that of women and Christian ministry. After all, the issue touches on matters of marriage, scriptural authority, sexuality, and church order.

Robert and Bonnidell Clouse, both teachers at Indiana State University, are no strangers to controversial questions. Robert Clouse has edited three books setting forth representative Christian views on the Millennium, war, and wealth and poverty. And in 1989, InterVarsity Press published their joint effort, Women in Ministry: Four Views. *Here they outline for us the three most common understandings of women's roles in ordained ministry. Then Kenneth Kantzer, dean of the Christianity Today Institute, offers cautious suggestions for churches planning to put their theologically trained women to work.*

One of the more pressing problems evangelicals wrestle with today concerns the ordination of women to the Christian ministry. Views on this issue can be summarized under three major divisions: the traditional approach, the egalitarian approach, and the plural ministry approach. Since the issue provokes strong visceral responses, let us merely summarize and clarify the thought that goes into each position—and at the same time hope to duck some of the crossfire.

The traditional approach

The traditional approach is compatible with male hierarchy, the social scheme that exists in the majority of the world's civilizations. Relegating women to a subordinate role leads to categorizing their abilities as different from those of men and to considering women as unfit for the positions from which they have been excluded, including that of being the preaching minister of a church. Samuel Johnson summed up the extreme form of this attitude in some memorable lines: "A woman's preaching is like a dog's walking on his hinder legs. It is not done well; but you are surprised to find it done at all."

The traditional view of women is that the Bible commands that they should be subordinate to men. Most Protestants have accepted this, both in the home and in the church. Historically, the two major Reformed bodies, the Lutherans and the Calvinists, did not allow women to be ordained, to preach, or to participate in the governing bodies of the church. The reasons for the opposition to women in ministry can be found in the traditional Protestant interpretation of Holy Scripture. References were often made to the fact that no disciple of Jesus was female and that none of the books of the Bible was written by a woman. But the major argument is drawn from a literal interpretation of certain Pauline texts, such as 1 Corinthians 11:2–16, 14:34–37, and 1 Timothy 2:8–15. According to the classical Protestant hermeneutic, the Bible must be interpreted through the writings of Paul, the capstone of God's written revelation. Thus it is logical that, despite examples of outstanding females mentioned in other parts of Scripture and the favorable statements of Jesus concerning the gifts and abilities of women, the statements of Paul should take precedence.

It is helpful for the sake of this discussion to review the major outline of Paul's statements. In 1 Corinthians 11–14 the apostle discusses aspects of public worship in the church. He writes in 11:2–16 (NIV):

> I praise you for remembering me in everything and for holding to the teachings, just as I passed them on to you.
>
> Now I want you to realize that the head of every man is Christ, and the head of the woman is man, and the head of Christ is God. Every man who prays or prophesies with his head covered dishonors his head. And every woman who prays or prophesies with her head uncovered dishonors her head—it is just as though her head were shaved. If a woman does not cover her head, she should have her hair cut off; and if it is a disgrace for a woman to have her hair cut or shaved off, she should cover her head. A man ought not to cover his head, since he is the image and glory of God; but a woman is the glory of man. For man did not come from woman, but woman from man; neither was man created for woman, but woman for man. For this reason, and because of the angels, the woman ought to have a sign of authority on her head.
>
> In the Lord, however, woman is not independent of man, nor is man independent of woman. For as woman came from man, so also man is born of woman. But everything comes from God. Judge for yourselves: Is it proper for a woman to pray to God with her head uncovered? Does not the very nature of things teach you that if a man has long hair, it is a disgrace to him, but that if a woman has long hair, it is her glory? For long hair is given to her as a covering. If anyone wants to be contentious about this, we have no other practice—nor do the churches of God.

This passage discusses the role of men and women in public assemblies. A sharp distinction is made between the sexes in appearance and in activity. Men are to have short hair and must not wear head coverings; women must have long hair and, in recognition of submission to God, must wear some sort of veil or hat. In addition to being subservient to God, a woman ought to submit to male domination. Among the reasons given for this is that man is the head of woman. Headship is a common metaphor for authority in Scripture. The Christian man's head is Christ, and the Christian woman's head is man, who represents to her Christ's head in God. Another argument is drawn from Creation, which states that man was created first and that woman was drawn from his side. A final reason for the subordination of females is that "because of the angels, the woman ought to have a sign of authority on her head" (v. 10). The sign of authority was a head covering, indicating subordination to male leadership. Angels are interested in this because they look after God's affairs on Earth, and women must not offend them by rebelling against the created order. One writer sums up the teaching of this passage: "Men are to exercise authority and take leadership in the church. Women should acknowledge that authority and support it in every Christian way, including dress and personal adornment when they attend public worship" (Robert Duncan Culver, in *Women in Ministry: Four Views*, ed. B. A. Clouse and R. G. Clouse, InterVarsity Press, 1989).

The second passage that is often used to justify the traditional exclusion of women from Christian ministry recommends that "women should remain silent in the churches. They are not allowed to speak, but must be in submission, as the Law says. If they want to inquire about something, they should ask their own husbands at home; for it is disgraceful for a woman to speak in the church. Did the word of God originate with you? Or are you the only people it has reached? If anyone thinks he is a prophet or spiritually gifted, let him acknowledge that what I am writing to you is the Lord's command" (1 Cor. 14:34–37, NIV). These verses, it is maintained, clearly forbid women to take a leadership role because it would be difficult to be silent and serve as a pastor, bishop, or district superintendent. The idea seems to be that a woman is forbidden to engage in the public act of speaking, whether to deliver a sermon, present a lecture, or even question the pastor of the church. The early church did not have Sunday schools, and consequently some who hold the traditional view would allow a woman to teach in these services. The passage counsels women to submit to male authority in a quiet and unprotesting manner. The apostle uses sarcasm to bolster his point as he reminds impudent and recalcitrant females that no woman had been a channel of God's revelation to the human race (v. 36). Thus women have no right to make changes in the ordinances and traditions of the church, including that of male leadership.

The final passage that is used to support the traditional view of the place of women in the church is 1 Timothy 2:8–15. Here Paul urges that

> men everywhere [ought to] lift up holy hands in prayer, without anger or disputing. I also want women to dress modestly, with decency and propriety, not with braided hair or gold or pearls or expensive clothes, but with good deeds, appropriate for women who profess to worship God. A woman should learn in quietness and full submission. I do not permit a woman to teach or to have authority over a man; she must be silent. For Adam was formed first, then Eve. And Adam was not the one deceived; it was the woman who was deceived and became a sinner. But women will be kept safe through childbirth, if they continue in faith, love and holiness with propriety (NIV).

These verses, drawn from one of the pastoral epistles, discuss the qualifications of ministers and the practice of public worship. The apostle instructs men to take leadership roles in the congregations, and he commands women to be subservient and dress in a modest manner. Women must avoid fancy hair styles, flashy jewelry, and lavish attire so that they will not draw attention to themselves and create a rift with the many poor people who cannot afford these refinements. The same commentator quoted above concludes: "Paul would have been speechless if he could have seen the leading ladies on current syndicated 'Christian' TV talk shows or on the platform of some fully Americanized Christian 'crusader.' Women are not to peddle their distinctly female wares at church. Nothing else in public life then or now seems to exclude excessive carnal display but one ought to be able to escape it at church." Paul indicates that there is a better way to achieve distinction in the community of faith than through a flashy appearance, and this is by performing good deeds and living a godly life. A woman's life of faith must be characterized by silence and submission.

Paul introduces a new argument for female subservience as he reminds his readers of the Genesis account of the fall of man. These early biblical passages teach that Eve was deceived by a half-truth, but Adam was persuaded to sin because of his affection for the woman. She was deceived, but he was not. The fact that Eve was so easily fooled indicates a lesser ability in comprehension, and this limitation explains why a woman must not teach or preach in church. To the traditionalist this seems to settle the argument concerning the basic difference between masculine and feminine natures. The dichotomy between the sexes furnishes the basis for male domination. The example of the catastrophe of Eden is a warning for all generations to heed whenever the sexes are tempted to repeat the folly of Adam and Eve and exchange their distinctive positions and functions.

There are other passages of Scripture that seem to contradict the traditional view of the role of women in the church. Two of the more familiar are Paul's statement that "there is neither Jew nor Greek, slave nor free, male nor female, for you are all one in Christ Jesus" (Gal. 3:28, NIV), and the account of Pentecost, when Peter quotes the prophet Joel to substantiate his preaching that "in the last days, God says, I will pour out my Spirit on all people. Your sons and daughters will prophesy, your young men will see visions, your old men will dream dreams" (Acts 2:17, NIV).

The Galatians passage is interpreted by the traditionalist to refer in a spiritual sense to the equality of salvation for all who are born again through faith in Jesus Christ. It is not thought to mean that everyone is equal in this life. Individuals obviously differ in their abilities, appearance, and opportunities. To believe that this verse supports the equality of women, therefore, is to take an ideal and apply it to a situation that cannot exist in an imperfect world. God is not an equal opportunity employer.

The traditionalist views the verses in Acts as reflecting a transitional period in the history of the church. The canon of Scripture was not complete at the time, and much of what is recorded in that book is not meant to be normative for the church. Miraculous jailbreaks, healing miracles, and speaking in tongues were given to support the early Christians as they broke away from Judaism. These unusual occurrences are not being repeated today. The same is true with women "prophesying."

It is interesting to note that recently many evangelical leaders have modified the strict traditionalist position. There are several ways in which this is done, but one of the more accepted methods is to allow women to participate in team ministries. It is possible in such a situation for women to teach men, if women approach the situation in a humble manner and if the director of the team is male. In these circumstances, a woman may exercise her gifts without claiming headship over men. As John Stott explains:

> If God endows women with spiritual gifts (which he does), and thereby calls them to exercise their gifts for the common good (which he does), then the Church must recognize God's gifts and calling, must make appropriate spheres of service available to women, and should "ordain" (that is, commission and authorize) them to exercise their God-given ministry, at least in team situations. Our Christian doctrines of Creation and Redemption tell us that God wants his gifted people to be fulfilled not frustrated, and his church to be enriched by their service.
>
> (*Issues Facing Christians Today*, Marshall, 1986, p. 254).

The egalitarian approach
Egalitarians believe that women as well as men should be ordained and serve as pastors of churches. Whereas the traditional view of male leadership argues from the created order of male-female relationships and focuses on Paul's writings, the egalitarians look to the life and teachings of Jesus and cite passages written by Paul that favor equality.

Jesus talked to the Samaritan woman as readily as he would have to a Jewish man. This both surprised and embarrassed the disciples. Had they known he had told her that true worship takes place in the mind and in the heart rather than in the temple at Jerusalem, they would have been doubly offended. Jesus' lack of social compliance and his resistance to the letter of the law marked him as a nonconformist both culturally and religiously.

The encounter with the woman at the well, recorded in John 4, was not the only time Jesus talked with a woman in public. Contrary to common Jewish practice, he often engaged women in conversation, treated them as equals, included them in his inner circle of friends, and revealed to them the deep truths of God's Word. He said it was more important for Mary, the sister of Lazarus and Martha, to listen to what he had to say than to be busy making preparations for guests. Luke 10:38–42 (NIV) reads:

> As Jesus and his disciples were on their way, he came to a village where a woman named Martha opened her home to him. She had a sister called Mary, who sat at the Lord's feet listening to what he said. But Martha was distracted by all the preparations that had to be made. She came to him and asked, "Lord, don't you care that my sister has left me to do the work by myself? Tell her to help me!"
>
> "Martha, Martha," the Lord answered, "you are worried and upset about many things, but only one thing is needed. Mary has chosen what is better, and it will not be taken away from her."

It is obvious from this passage that the stereotypical image of woman's work and man's work, woman's interests and man's interests, so much a part of first-century Palestine and still held by many people today, was not Jesus' approach. The traditional hierarchy of men as rulers and women as domestics cannot be found in Jesus' teachings. The egalitarians feel that if Jesus did not hold to gender differences, then we should not hold to them either.

Egalitarians also look to the writings of the apostle Paul to show that women as well as men are qualified to be ministers or pastors. A favorite passage is Galatians 3:28 where Paul writes: "There is neither . . . male nor female . . . in Christ Jesus" (NIV). Women were prominent figures in the early church. They were coworkers with the men, opened their homes to the gospel, and functioned in the capacity of deacon or minister. They were called apostles and were given the gifts of the Holy Spirit. No distinction was made between "male gifts" and "female gifts." All are one in Christ. If Paul, stating that all are sons of God through faith and all are baptized into Christ, did not differentiate in his day between Jew and Greek, slave and free, or male and female (Gal. 3:26–28), then we in the twentieth century should not differentiate either. Both men and women must be given the opportunity to reach their full potential to serve Christ in whatever capacity they feel called.

But Paul did not always equate the role of men and women, and egalitarians must respond to those verses written by Paul that are used by the traditionalists as the basis for their beliefs. As we have seen, the traditional stance focuses on Paul's letter to the Corinthians in which a woman is told to have her head covered when she prays or prophesies (1 Cor. 11:2–16) and she is to remain silent, "for it is disgraceful for a woman to speak in church" (1 Cor. 14:35). Furthermore, Paul wrote to Timothy that "a woman should learn in quietness and full submission" and not teach or have authority over a man (1 Tim. 2:11–12). It follows directly that if a woman is not to teach or even say anything during the church service, she cannot be the preaching minister or pastor of the church.

The egalitarian answer is that these stipulations were given to particular churches of that time and should not be considered normative for all congregations and for all generations. Homosexuality was prevalent in Corinth, and the long, ornately styled hair of the males and the closely cropped hair of the females distracted the worshipers. Prostitution was also practiced in Corinth, and although the women in the church no longer lived in sin, they brought their loud, raucous behavior into the service, and this was what required the mandate that they be silent. Paul had just said that women would pray and prophesy (1 Cor. 11:5), and thus to tell them to be "silent" would not make sense unless it referred to such specific incidents.

In the 1 Timothy passage, women are not only to learn in silence and not teach or have authority over men; they are not to braid their hair or wear jewelry or expensive clothes. If applied today, this would mean a woman could not teach Sunday school or sing in the choir or wear a wedding ring. Egalitarians say that if traditionalists want to be literalists in their interpretation of certain passages of Scripture, then they should be consistent and treat all Scripture in the same way. They clearly do not do this. Traditionalists, like other believers, select specific verses for emphasis and ignore other verses they deem to be less important. If one insists that women are to dress and act in the way prescribed in the epistles to the Corinthians and to Timothy, then one should also insist that women not be missionaries, braid their hair, or wear any kind of jewelry. A strictly literal interpretation would mean that both men and women today would conform to dietary restrictions based on whether food had been offered to idols, that widows could not become church members until they reached the age of 60, that believers would greet one another with a holy kiss rather than with a handshake, that believers would wash each other's feet, and that all would be required to drink wine as an aid to digestion. The point is made that until traditionalists are willing to be consistent rather than selective in their literalism, it is difficult to take their views seriously.

Egalitarians prefer to follow Jesus' example of putting "the spirit of the law" before "the letter of the law." They welcome changes in the society that result in greater freedom for the individual, for this creates a milieu in which each person, male or female, is more apt to reach his or her full potential, including the potential to serve God and to further his cause. That change within the society affects the church cannot be disputed. All of us conform to a degree to the customs of the day. We go to church in suits and dresses; first-century believers (both men and women) wore robes. We arrive in cars; they came on foot or on horseback. We bring our Bibles; they did not have Bibles nor could they read. We have Sunday school for our youth; they did not appear to make special provisions for the teaching of small children. We do not consider these differences between ourselves and the early Christians to be spiritual or moral matters. Rather, they are simply differences in style, a natural consequence of the passage of time in societies not isolated from the rest of the world. The spirit of the law takes into consideration these changes, and the law is not violated. The letter of the law does not allow for change, and thus it stifles the creative potential within each believer and renders him or her a less effective member of the body of Christ.

Furthermore, the spirit of the law looks to those principles that, though their practice may vary from place to place and from one generation to another, in themselves are universal and invariant and stand the test of time. How do we recognize these principles or highest standards? Writes Alvera Mickelsen of Bethel College: "Highest standards were emphasized by Jesus Christ (and sometimes by Paul) and were often plainly stated as the highest standard. For example, Jesus stated flatly that the Golden Rule was the highest standard" (*Women in Ministry: Four Views*): "In everything, do to others what you would have them do to you, for this sums up the Law and the Prophets" (Matt. 7:12, NIV). Another standard is, "Love the Lord your God with all your heart and with all your soul, and with all your mind" (Matt. 22:37, NIV).

Still another is Paul's principle of being "all things to all men so that by all possible means I might save some"(1 Cor. 9:22, NIV). Paul says in this passage that when he is with the Jews he becomes like a Jew; when he is with those who are under the law he becomes as one under the law; when he is with those who are not under the law he becomes as one not under the law. One must act in a way that does not make the gospel offensive. In the pagan world of the first century, this meant that women should dress and behave in ways that were acceptable to the social order of the time. A woman teaching in the church would constitute a moral problem and bring shame on the gospel of Christ. As Walter Liefeld of Trinity Evangelical Divinity School has written: "Today it is just the reverse. A society that accepts women as corporation executives and university presidents will find it difficult to listen to a church that silences them" (*Women in Ministry: Four Views*).

How Shall We Respond to Women Who Are Ready to Minister?

Kenneth S. Kantzer

Many women are justifiably becoming frustrated at their church's lack of sensitivity in dealing with the issue. Church leaders experience similar turmoil as they seek biblical solutions to the problem. They recognize that even if their previous exegesis of Scripture referring to women was wrong, any change would be uncomfortable for their congregations. And if they conclude that Scripture really *does* forbid women from assuming an active role in the life of the church, adhering to the Word may initially alienate many in their congregations. Add to this the fact that, according to a 1980 survey, only 5 to 10 percent of all men genuinely support women's efforts toward equality—and one understands why the church cannot ignore the issue.

The older and established churches have traditionally refused to ordain women and have argued that the Bible does not permit a woman to preach or teach. Within the last two decades, however, these mainline denominations have moved more in the direction of ordaining women for pastoral ministry. Newer churches—the early Methodists, many Anabaptist sects, the revivalist churches on the frontier in America, Holiness churches, the Pentecostal movement, several parachurch ministries, and overseas missions carried on by evangelical churches—have historically made provisions for women to assume positions of leadership. Yet in many of these groups, few women have actually risen through the ranks to become leaders.

The biblical case against women preachers and teachers rests on a few well-known passages (for example, 1 Timothy 2 and 1 Corinthians 14). We believe that none of these passages rules out the ordination of women as preachers, teachers, or leaders in the church.

But what about the question of prudence? If Scripture makes no universal rule against women teachers and leaders, is it ever wise to deny such roles to women just because they are women? Yes. Though "all things are lawful, not all things are expedient." Sometimes, for the sake of the "weaker" brother, we must forgo using legitimate freedoms. Christians have often practiced such self-restraint, especially in missionary efforts where cultural customs must be respected. It is seldom wise or expedient to run roughshod over another's values or beliefs, especially in areas of disputed biblical interpretation. In order not to offend others who are convinced that the Bible forbids women to teach, in certain situations we must choose not to ordain women for the sake of the gospel.

This does not mean we set aside our concern for the status of women in the church. If anything, we must intensify our efforts to bring others to a proper understanding of Scripture. But we do this with grace and sensitivity. We must consistently teach what the Scriptures really say on this important point. Further, it is the special responsibility of men to make the church aware of this teaching and to give solid support to women who possess gifts of teaching and leadership.

A most difficult question remains: What shall we do about the increasing number of highly gifted and well-trained women seeking to use their gifts and to minister in the church?

The answer would seem to be very simple: If Scripture does not forbid, ordain them and encourage them to teach in the church.

Unfortunately, we do not live in an ideal world where simple answers are always best. We carry the baggage of history. For centuries the church has allowed its view of women to be warped by the society around it. Generally it has not overthrown the social structures in which it carries on its witness, but it seeks to alleviate their worst features and influence them for good.

So it has been with the role of women. American women are among the most liberated women in the world. Many Christian women (as well as men) sincerely believe that this new-found freedom will destroy the home and damage the Christian nurture of our young. Others are convinced that the Bible flatly prohibits women from teaching men. Still others argue that, for cultural reasons, a woman ought not to be given senior roles in teaching and leadership in the church.

We must not disregard these sincerely held views. But neither dare we ignore the immense potential of the divinely given skills that many women possess to teach and lead the church. On the contrary, we must encourage them in their exercise of those gifts. Where necessary, we must urge them to seek avenues that are less disturbing to the peace of the church. As women exercise their gifts and confirm their divine call to ministry, the church profits. It loses its fears and becomes more receptive to the leadership of women in additional areas. It is then driven to re-examine its exegesis to see if its universal prohibition of women teachers and leaders is not more derived from ancient prejudices than from the biblical texts.

While we support this cautious approach, we urge the church to do all it can to resolve this issue, and to proceed in earnest. The church suffers from a dearth of solid, scripturally sound teaching and from a dangerous void of leadership. Women could supply more and more of these crucial services were we more open to their ministry. Our failure to use their skills becomes more and more irrational in the light of the role of women in the society around us. Throughout society, women are proving that they have the ability to teach and to lead. Margaret Thatcher can instruct and guide millions of citizens—men and women alike—throughout Great Britain and the Commonwealth; but even if she possessed a vital Christian experience, she could not be a deacon in many of our evangelical churches. And the church is the loser. It loses not only because it cannot avail itself of the tremendous gifts God has given to women like Margaret Thatcher. It loses also because increasingly it is turning our finest women away from a church that they see not as the body of Christ where we are all one in the Lord, but as a male preserve that selfishly seeks to cling to worldly power in the name of Christ. We twist the Scripture to suit our own ends.

What shall we then say? We must continue to turn to the infallible Holy Scriptures that instruct us so we may wisely and faithfully serve Christ and his church in our day.

Chapter 8

CAN I
REALLY TRUST
THE BIBLE?

Kenneth S. Kantzer

In 1978, theologian Kenneth S. Kantzer, then editor of CHRISTIANITY
TODAY, *joined forces with other evangelical leaders in the International
Council on Biblical Inerrancy to hold the first inerrancy "summit" and
issue the Chicago Statement on Biblical Inerrancy. In 1987, with a
sense of "mission accomplished," Kantzer participated in the council's
final congress and dissolution.*

*But Kantzer's lifetime of prayerful reflection on the nature of Scrip-
ture is not finished. Here are his thoughts on the importance of
believing in a trustworthy Scripture.*

Karl Barth, the greatest theologian of the twentieth century, was dead right when he wrote that "Christianity has always been and only been a living religion when it is not ashamed to be actually and seriously a book religion." He was equally correct when he defined the essence of Christianity in the simple verse of the cradle hymn: Jesus loves me, this I know, for the Bible tells me so. No other story is quite so wonderful; and no other book is quite so important to humankind, therefore, as the Bible.

But why do we accept its authority? What sort of authority is it?

Two great purposes
The first purpose of the Bible is to introduce us to the Savior and his salvation. This Book brings to us the gospel—the good news that the infinite God loves us human sinners, loves us enough to break through whatever barriers stand between himself and us, to forgive our sin and win us back into the joy of an eternal fellowship with himself and with all that is good and just and true. This is the essence of Christianity. All else serves merely to display the jewel, that it might sparkle more brilliantly on its mounting.

In 2 Timothy 3:14–15, the apostle Paul spells out for us this first great purpose: "The holy Scriptures ... are able to make you wise unto salvation through faith which is in Christ Jesus" (NKJV). The Bible is, first of all, a witness to Christ; it leads men and women to him and to his salvation. The primary object of our Christian faith and the rock-bottom foundation on which our Christian faith rests, is Jesus Christ. And this is the focal center of the entire Bible—both Old and New Testaments. Contrary to Marcion in ancient times, and Schleiermacher and his liberal followers more recently, the Old Testament is indispensable to Christian faith. Its importance to the gospel runs through almost every page of the New Testament. Our Lord rebuked the Jewish leaders for their lack of insight into the real meaning of the Old Testament. "You diligently study the Scriptures. ... [But] these are the Scriptures that testify about me" (John 5:39, NIV). And the apostles reinforce the same theme. In 1 Corinthians 15:1–4, Paul defines the gospel: "How ... Christ died for our sins according to the Scriptures." And Timothy found the Savior through the Old Testament.

But when we have found the Savior, we need instruction so we may know how to live lives that will please him and serve him. The second great purpose of the Bible, therefore, is to instruct us in Christian faith. Paul discusses this in the same passage in which he sets forth the first principle. "All Scripture is inspired by God and profitable for teaching, for reproof, for correction, and for training in righteousness, that the man of God may be complete, equipped for every good work" (2 Tim. 3:16–17).

In the Old Testament, Jehovah God commissioned and sent his prophets to guide his covenant people in the way of God in order that they might serve him, live good and useful lives, and advance his kingdom. Similarly, under the New Covenant, our Lord commissioned his apostles. "He that heareth you heareth me," Jesus declared to his disciples (Luke 10:16). "He that receiveth you, receiveth me" (Matt. 10:40). He promised Peter that he would be the rock on which he, Christ, would build his church. And he gave Peter the keys of the kingdom of heaven for the binding and loosing of humans on Earth (Matt. 16:18–19).

This same power and authority our Lord also gave to the entire body of apostles (Matt. 18:18; John 20:23). And for that purpose he promised them the Spirit, who would teach them what they should speak (Matt. 10:20), bring to their minds what he had said to them in his earthly ministry (John 14:26) and guide them into all truth (John 16:13). The apostles were to function as representatives of Jesus Christ. They were granted full authority to speak for their Master. For the Christian, therefore, the authority of the Scripture is a matter of obedience to the Lord of the church.

The inspiration of Scripture

The Scriptures are the means by which Jesus Christ, through the Holy Spirit, provides instruction and guidance for his people. The apostle Paul speaks of the biblical writings as *theopneustia*, or God-breathed. The Scripture is produced by the Spirit of God. Evangelicals employ a number of terms to describe this view of inspiration: "verbally inspired," "infallible," "inerrant." Each carries with it an aspect of truth, but each also is liable to misinterpretation and thus may lead to a faulty view of the nature of biblical inspiration.

"Verbal inspiration," for example, has been heavily attacked because it seems to imply a dictation method. It is true that the

Reformers (and some before their day) occasionally employed the Latin word *dictare* (to dictate) to describe their understanding of biblical inspiration. Invariably, however, the Reformers displayed no intention of denying a genuine human authorship of Scripture. They only wanted to show that God had indeed guided the entire production of Scripture and that the message and the words used to convey the message were under his sovereign control. What Scripture says is what God wished to say, as much as though he had dictated it according to the pattern of a boss and a stenographer.

But what sort of dictation is this? The full and complete humanity of the Bible shouts at us from every page. This must be taken with full seriousness. The biblical writers use their own language. They write from the context of their own culture. Their style is peculiarly their own. Their themes are those dear to their heart. Moses differs from Isaiah, John from Matthew, Paul from James. No literary genre that is appropriate for good human literature is necessarily inappropriate for the biblical authors. From first to last, the entire Bible is a human book and can only be understood and rightly interpreted as a thoroughly human book.

The humanity of Scripture is no new invention of the twentieth century. It is embedded in the Bible's own view of itself and has with rare exceptions been recognized by the church throughout its history. The words "Moses commanded," "David wrote," and "Isaiah says" appear side by side with the "word of God says," "the Holy Spirit says," and "Isaiah by the Spirit says" with no sense of incompatibility or contradiction. The message and the written medium through which it comes to us are alike ascribed to the human author and to the divine source. Paul in 1 Corinthians 2 speaks of the revelation that came to the apostolic witnesses directly from God himself (2:6–11). This revelation is precisely what the apostle handed over to the church. And he communicated this revelation to the church in words that were not merely his own but were guided and chosen by the Spirit of God (2:13). Peter, in his epistle, teaches that scriptural prophecy is not merely a private interpretation; rather, the prophets wrote as they were moved and guided by the Spirit of God. For this reason their word is "sure" and we "do well to pay attention" to it (2 Pet. 1:19–21, NIV).

To some, this view of the Bible seems to present an insoluble problem. How can God sovereignly control the writing of the Bible down to the very words that compose it if the Bible is truly a human book, stemming from the mind and heart of the human author? This is not a problem from the viewpoint of the God of the Bible. The God of some people is not big enough to run a peanut stand. But the Bible presents us with a true theism—a God who is sovereign over all and who therefore can work all things together for good to them who love him. He can do so, moreover, without destroying human freedom or human responsibility for sin. If God can use the freedom of a wicked king like Nebuchadnezzar to secure his own ends, surely he can use his own prophets or apostles to convey exactly the message he wishes without destroying the freedom and true human authorship of biblical writing.

Thus, when God chooses to give us his great teaching on love in 1 Corinthians 13, he is not limited to verbal dictation in order to say exactly what he wishes to communicate. Rather, he calls Saul from his mother's womb, rears him in the Roman city of Tarsus, trains him under the great rabbi Gamaliel, meets him on the road to Damascus, sends him to Arabia for a time of orientation, fills him with the Holy Spirit, guides him on his missionary tour, and brings him face to face with the problems of the gentile church at Corinth—all just at the right moment so that, out of the white heat of his own experience, Paul freely says exactly what God wishes him to say. There is no problem of inspiration here; it is a problem of theism.

Christians have often pointed to the analogy between the two natures in Christ and the divine and human in Scripture. Jesus Christ is thoroughly and completely human. He is also truly divine—the Second Person of the triune God. And just as his full humanity and his full deity must be preserved in all their integrity within the unity of one single person, Jesus Christ, so the full human authority and responsibility of the scriptural author and the fully divine responsibility for what Scripture says, and therefore, its consequent divine authority as well, must be preserved in all their integrity.

The terms *infallible* and *inerrant* as applied to Scripture are loosely synonymous. Yet *infallible* is the stronger term; it denotes that the Scripture is *incapable* of error. *Inerrant* is a weaker term, noting only that the Scripture does not err. A newspaper can be inerrant, but it is never infallible.

Unfortunately, both terms are occasionally used differently from the way they have traditionally been employed. Both are sometimes limited by qualifying phrases such as "in religious faith and ethical practice," or "in specifically revelational matters." There is, of course, no problem in using either term in such a restricted way, *as long as* the qualifying phrases are properly noted. Recently, however, the terms have been used by some writers, without the qualifying phrases, to mean that only parts of the Bible are preserved from error. This leads only to confusion. Without the qualifiers most people rightly understand the terms to be used in an absolute sense, as they have normally been employed in the past.

That this is the way such terms have been used by the church in the past is really beyond question. Speaking for the ancient Greek church, Irenaeus wrote: "The Scriptures are indeed perfect, since they were spoken by the Word of God and His Spirit." Augustine, representing the ancient Western church and the medieval church, declared: "As to all other writings . . . I do not accept their teaching as true on the mere ground of the opinion held by them; but . . . the canonical writings are free from error." At the time of the Reformation Luther only affirmed the mainstream of historical Christianity when he wrote, "Holy Scriptures cannot err." Calvin was no less explicit in his references to the Bible as the "pure word of God" and as "the infallible rule of His holy truth." Indeed, one of his original charges against the heretic Servetus was that he had written a book ascribing a geographical error to Holy Scripture. And from this charge Servetus freed himself only by pointing out that the book in question had a dual author and that he was not responsible for the statement indicating an error in the Bible. John Wesley, fighting against the incipient rationalism of his day, exclaimed: "If there be one error in Scripture, there might as well be a thousand. It would not be the truth of God." And Kirsopp Lake, professor at Harvard University, stated: "How many were there, for instance, in Christian churches in the eighteenth century who doubted the infallible inspiration of all Scripture? A few, perhaps, but very few. . . . It is we [liberals] who have departed from the tradition. . . . The Bible and the *corpus theologicum* of the church are on the fundamentalist side "

Jesus' view of Scripture
The primary case for the complete truthfulness of Holy Scripture rests on the familiar passages bearing to us the instruction of our

Lord. In Mark 7:6–13 he explicitly repudiates the teachings of his contemporaries and sets the Holy Scripture in sharp contrast to it. He then equates what Moses said with what God says. What Moses commanded is the Word of God. In similar fashion, Jesus (and following him, his apostles) cites the Old Testament with the introduction "God says," or "the Holy Spirit by Isaiah the prophet says," or "the Spirit by the mouth of David spoke." Accordingly, we are not surprised when in the Sermon on the Mount Jesus defends the complete authority of Scripture as opposed to the faulty teaching of others that was based on their misinterpretations of the Old Testament. "Do not think," he writes, "that I have come to destroy the law and the prophets." In fact, our Lord objected to the teaching of these leaders on the very grounds that it subverted the law and the prophets. It was his desire to protect the full integrity of the truth of Scripture that led him to reject their traditions. He therefore notes: "One jot or tittle shall in no wise depart from the law, till all be fulfilled" (Matt. 5:17–19). And he is speaking not of a prediction of the future but of a command that must be obeyed.

In Luke 16:17 he adds that no part of the law can be set aside as useless. In John 10:35, again in controversy with religious leaders, he states: "The Scripture cannot be broken." He encourages the disciples "to believe all that the prophets have spoken" (Luke 24:25). In our Lord's view, the whole of Scripture is of one piece. It is, in every part of it, the Word of God that comes to us as divine truth without any error whatsoever.

Subjective and objective illumination
Belief in the verbal and infallible inspiration of Holy Scripture, moreover, does not, as some fear, suggest a wooden and over-literal mode of interpretation. To speak of the verbal and infallible inspiration of the Bible is only to assert its complete truth. In one sense we should interpret the Bible just as any other book, because it, too, is a thoroughly human book. To understand it rightly we must understand the grammar, syntax, and historical and cultural framework in which it was written. We must ascertain the intended meaning of the original author in the particular situation to which he was referring. What the author really said then stands as the authoritative message that comes to us from God.

But in another sense, the Bible is quite different from other books.

It is God who addresses us in the Bible. If it commands us to do something, we are to obey. If it asks a question, we are to answer. If it makes an assertion, we are to believe it to be so.

Moreover, it is not just the case that God spoke these words through his apostles and prophets to a people who lived millennia ago. The one who spoke them there and then is also the omnipresent, ever-living God. He dwells in each one of his children. He has promised to accompany his Word, open our minds to its truth, and then speak to us today what he said through his ancient prophets and apostles long ago. The response of the believer today should be the same as that of Samuel to whom the Word of the Lord came three millennia past: "Speak, Lord, for thy servant heareth" (1 Sam. 3:10).

Paul describes the work of the Spirit enabling us to receive and use the revelation that God has given. The Bible refers to this work specifically as "illumination," and at times as "revelation." This subjective aspect of the present work of the Holy Spirit is the necessary complement to its objective inspiration.

When the subjective illumination of Scripture is ignored, the Bible is liable to become a dead book and to seem irrelevant to the life of the believer today. The present Spirit convinces us that the Bible is in truth not just an ancient book, but the very Word of God spoken long ago for our benefit. In this, the Spirit may or may not use evidences as he sovereignly deems appropriate. And he does what in principle no amount of objective evidence could ever do—he opens up eyes to see. Only the indwelling Holy Spirit can give us personal certainty. William Cowper puts it aptly in his hymn: "The Spirit breathes upon the Word, and brings the truth to sight."

The Spirit also opens up our minds to its true meaning in the context in which it was given and guides us to its present application to us—the meaning for me in my particular situation in which God is leading me. The Bible has one authorial meaning—the meaning originally intended by the author. This comes with infallible authority. But it has many applications or personal meanings, as varied as are the individual believers whom the Spirit of God is instructing.

Through the present work of the Holy Spirit, the Bible becomes an effective guide for all believers in their divergent problems and the diverse life situations each one must face. No doubt these applications or personal meanings are at times mistaken. They are, after all, meanings made by fallible and sinful humans, always subject to error. Yet we are saved from drifting too far from what is true and good because we have an infallible standard by which to test our fallible interpretations of the text and our fallible applications and personal meanings according to which we conduct our life and thought.

Is the text inerrant?

Of course it is necessary to note that we do not hold an infallible text in our hand when, for example, we turn the pages of the New International Version. Nor, for that matter, do we have the infallible text in Nestle's twenty-fourth edition of the Greek New Testament, or in the Kittel text of the Hebrew Old Testament.

Some have argued that this destroys any value of an inerrant original. Emil Brunner, for example, pokes fun at those who get hot and bothered about the inerrancy of a Bible "X"—the great unknown. All our actual copies are fallible. Why not, therefore, be satisfied to defend the general truth of the Bible, if that is all we have anyway? But Brunner's own practice belies what he says. The fact is, we do possess this correct and infallible text in most cases (some would claim 99 percent of the text). And the difference an infallible original can make is clearly to be discerned in the case of Brunner. He had no doubt that the Virgin Birth was clearly part of the original text of both Matthew and Luke. But because he believed the original text to be fallible, he could reject what it said. Both Brunner (and other errantists) and evangelical inerrantists begin with a fallible text in their hands. And they both use the same objective data of textual criticism to arrive at the correct text. Amazingly enough, they almost always agree. Most strict evangelicals, for example, use the Greek and Hebrew texts prepared by unbelieving scholars and do so without serious reservations. They interpret the text on the basis of the same grammatical, historical, and cultural data as do those who hold to an errant original.

The difference lies in this: When evangelicals get to the end of the process, the degree of probability that they have the correct text and the degree of probability that they have the correct interpretation of that text is precisely the degree of probability that they have the very truth of the living God to guide their life and thought. For

Brunner and other errantists, these same probabilities give them only the degree of assurance that they have what an ancient writer thought to be the truth. If Brunner wants to know the truth, he must put the biblical teaching through a sieve.

It is exactly this additional sieve that leaves him in deep trouble. Most suggested criteria are thoroughly subjective in the sense that no objective data can be presented as to why one must believe this part of the Bible while feeling free to reject other parts. Even more destructive is the fact that our Lord himself gave us no method by which to determine what we should receive and what we should reject from the Bible. Quite the reverse: He commanded us to receive all of it, down to the very jot and tittle of what was written. Naturally, this lays a serious burden upon all disciples of Christ to make sure that they intepret Scripture honestly and fairly. The Bible is not a scientific textbook. Neither is it a sort of neutral history of human culture. It is not always precise in its language. Jesus did not teach any of these things. Rather, he taught that the Bible is wholly true and never says what is false in any area. All he promised is that the Scripture is all true, is worthy of our trust, and provides an adequate guide for life.

Opposition to infallibility
The doctrine of the infallible authority of Holy Scripture has not been without opposition. Until modern times that opposition largely came from outside the church. In the last century, however, it mounted up within the church. Today it is safe to say that the infallibility of the Bible is a minority view within the nominal church of Christ. Opponents have argued that it is a dangerous view because it suggests that one error found in Scripture would destroy the whole edifice of Christian faith. This is not true, of course, any more than that one error in a modern text on U.S. history would destroy our confidence in the existence of the United States of America.

The proof of an error in Scripture would not destroy belief in the deity of Christ or the gospel or the general truth of Christian faith. However, it would destroy our confidence that the Bible is a completely trustworthy authority and guide to the teaching of Christ and thus would be a great loss to the Christian church. We could no longer build our theology on the teaching of the whole of the Bible and would instead have to develop a new method for building theology. As a result, we would undoubtedly have a new theology.

Are there errors?
A more significant charge is that there *are* errors in the Bible. But this is not easy to prove. Those who have sought to establish errors in the Bible have generally not been able to turn to the unquestioned teachings of modern science or facts from history that contradict biblical teaching. As a final proof that the Bible contains errors, they have turned to those puzzling passages between Kings and Chronicles, between the history of Genesis and Acts, or in the parallel accounts of the four Gospels.

Such apparent discrepancies, however, are not newly discovered problems for the church. They were clearly known and understood by the church when it formulated its doctrine of an infallible Scripture. In the ancient church Jerome and Augustine discussed them at length, and, in fact, they remain in many cases as unsolved problems even to this day. They are, it is important to note, just what one would expect to find in an inerrant book written over many cultures, covering thousands of years, involving different types and personalities of authors writing independently about many diverse events.

Some time ago the mother of a dear friend of ours was killed. We first learned of her death through a trusted mutual friend, who reported that our friend's mother had been standing on the street corner waiting for a bus, had been hit by another bus passing by, was fatally injured, and died a few minutes later. Shortly thereafter, we learned from the grandson of the dead woman that she had been involved in a collision, was thrown from the car in which she was riding, and was killed instantly. The boy was quite certain of his facts, relayed them clearly, and stated that he had secured his information directly from his mother—the daughter of the woman who had been killed. No further information was forthcoming from either source. Which would you believe?

We trusted both our friends, but we certainly could not assemble the data in a single sequence. Much later, upon further inquiry, we were able to talk to our friend and her son in our living room. There, quietly and slowly, we probed for a harmonization. We learned that the grandmother had been waiting for a bus, was hit by another bus, and was critically injured. She had been picked up by a passing car to rush her to the hospital—but in the haste, the car in which she was being transported to the hospital collided with another car. She was thrown from the car and died instantly. I submit that this story from my own experience presents no greater difficulty than that of any recorded in the Gospels, not even excepting the two divergent accounts of the death of Judas.

Such coincidences occur repeatedly. They are inherent in independent accounts of any event. The only significant difference between this story and the accounts of the four Evangelists is the fact that we cannot cross-examine the gospel witnesses. We live 2,000 years too late. We cannot say, "Now see here, Matthew and Luke, what really happened at the death of Judas?" We must treat both Matthew and Luke as friends and trust what they say even when we cannot explain exactly how their divergent accounts are to be reconciled. It is unreasonable to refuse to believe two reliable witnesses simply because we are unable to furnish a complete harmony of all they say.

At the end of my training for the doctorate, I had cultivated a large, refrigerated freight car's worth of unsolved problems. I was confident they could be solved, but I was equally confident that I did not know how they could be harmonized. It is important in such cases that we do not sweep the problems permanently out of sight. Rather, we should place them in reserve, bring them out from time to time, and seek to solve them, always with the recognition that it is reasonable to place our confidence in the complete truth of Scripture even though we may not be able to harmonize every alleged contradiction. Over the years, most of the items in my freight car of unsolved problems have been brought out and solutions have been found. But at the same time, I must confess that I have a new carload almost equally large, a new set of different problems. And I expect this process to continue until I depart this life.

Historical criticism

What about historical criticism? No evangelical objects to the historical criticism of the Bible in a legitimate sense of that term. In fact, evangelicals also seek to investigate the author and the date, background, and culture in which the biblical writings were produced. Only then can the truth that God has chosen to reveal in them be properly understood. What evangelicals object to is the purpose for which historical criticism is often engaged in. Too frequently, the purpose is not to discover what the biblical author is really trying to say but rather to psychoanalyze the biblical author and to reconstruct a secular historical background of the biblical literature. Evangelicals are interested in these things, too. But their primary motive for engaging in such criticism is to learn precisely what the biblical author says in the confidence that, when they do so, they are also learning what God has to say to his people today.

Evangelicals also object to the particular method most historical critics employ. They eliminate the miraculous. Most contemporary scholars, in fact, stretch the biblical material over a Procrustean bed of the naturalistic evolution of religion. This is not historical criticism. It is a philosophy of history in which the critic chooses a world view, and in this case, it is a world view quite different from anything that can be called Christian.

Christians are supernaturalists. They believe that miracles can and do happen. When acceptance of a miracle provides a more coherent picture of the data, evangelicals accept the miracle without qualms. A quick look at almost any survey of the history of Israel not written by a Christian supernaturalist will quickly show how an antisupernatural presupposition radically distorts one's view of biblical history, its truth, and ultimately the divine authority of Holy Scripture.

Evangelicals have no problem with the study of the origin and background of biblical writings, and that is what biblical criticism purports to investigate. They do object to the methodology used by nonsupernaturalist biblical critics, and they object to the conclusions to which many critics come. Evangelicals are open to all views of biblical origins and backgrounds that do not flatly contradict the data of the biblical material itself.

Of course, if the Book of Deuteronomy claims to set forth a collection of addresses by the lawgiver Moses at the time of the entrance of the Jewish people into the land of Palestine, one who believes in the inerrancy of Scripture cannot also hold that the Book of Deuteronomy was foisted by deception on the people of Israel centuries later in order to cement the power of the Levitical priesthood. Likewise, if a pastoral epistle claims to be written by the apostle Paul, one who holds to inerrancy cannot also believe that this was a piece of literature concocted long after Paul's death to try to strengthen the authority of second-century bishops.

A consistent and obedient Christianity

The importance of the view of the Bible and its inspiration can scarcely be overestimated. It is true that biblical infallibility is not essential to the existence of Christian faith. Faith in Jehovah existed long before there was an Old Testament, and faith in Jesus Christ came into being before any book of the New Testament was written. No instructed evangelical, moreover, would suggest that belief in an infallible Bible is necessary for salvation or for a godly life. C. S. Lewis did not believe in an infallible Bible, and I shall be hanging around heaven a long time before I shall ever get near enough to the throne of God to see C. S. Lewis.

Neither is belief in the infallible authority of Scripture a requirement for church membership. The church is a body of those who profess faith in Christ and seek to live under his lordship. It is for believers only, but it is for all believers who give a creditable profession of their faith in Christ.

Yet belief in an infallible Bible is essential to a consistent Christianity. Individuals may survive without commitment to the complete authority of Scripture and can, no doubt with great inconsistency, pick from the Bible what they choose to believe. The lordship of Christ, however, requires obedience to the teaching of the prophets and the apostles. Our Lord accepted Scripture as the guide for his own life and taught his followers to do the same. Belief in the authority of the Bible, therefore, is important for leaders within the church. We build our theology upon the whole Bible under the instruction of Christ. If we turn from his instruction at this point to pick and choose from the Bible what we believe, we shall necessarily have to build a new theology. And it will not be the theology that the church in the past has derived from Scripture.

The main reason for accepting the infallible authority of Scripture must once again be reasserted. The real Jesus, the only Jesus for whom we have any evidence whatsoever, believed that the Bible was true and that it was the very Word of God. He commanded his disciples to believe it and obey it. He rebuked those who disregarded it or sought to interpret away its obvious instructions. And he held its teachings binding over himself.

The real issue for us today is: Is Jesus Christ Lord? Only when we have answered this question—the most basic of all questions—are we prepared to answer the further question: Is the Bible the infallible Word of God, the authoritative guide for our life and thought? Our answer to this second question is the way to become obedient and faithful and useful disciples of the Lord Christ.

Chapter 9

WILL A LOVING GOD REALLY CONDEMN PEOPLE TO HELL? IS CHRIST THE ONLY WAY?

J. I. Packer

Non-Christians object to the idea that those who have never heard the gospel will be condemned to hell. Thus some Christians have ended up teaching universalism—the belief that everyone, sooner or later, will be reconciled to God and saved by him.

But if all will eventually be saved, why should they sacrifice to become Christians in this life? Why, indeed, should we endure hardship to evangelize them? First, J. I. Packer, author of Evangelism and the Sovereignty of God *(IVP), takes a careful look at universalism's appeal and problems. Then Roger R. Nicole examines what the Bible says about the fate of the impenitent.*

The problem of individual human destinies has always pressed hard upon thoughtful Christians who take the Bible seriously, for Scripture affirms these three things:

1. The *reality* of hell as a state of eternal destructive punishment in which God's judicial retribution for sin is directly experienced.

2. The *certainty* of hell for all who choose it by rejecting Jesus Christ and his offer of eternal life.

3. The *justice* of hell as a fit divine infliction upon humanity for our lawless and cruel deeds.

It was, to be sure, hell-deserving sinners whom Jesus came to save, and all who put their trust in him may know themselves forgiven, justified, and accepted forever—and thus delivered from the wrath to come. But what of those who lack this living faith? Those who are not just hypocrites in the church, about whose destiny Christ is very clear, but "good pagans" who lived before the Incarnation, or who through no fault of their own never heard the Christian message, or who met it only in an incomplete and distorted form? Or what about those who lived in places (modern Albania, for instance) where Christianity was a capital offense, or who suffered from ethnonationalistic or socio-cultural conditioning against the faith, or who were so resentful of Christians for hurting them in one way or another that they were never emotionally free for serious thought about Christian truth? Are they all necessarily lost?

Mixed answers

To this question Christians have given mixed answers:

• Some have maintained that all unbelievers go to hell because, being sinners like everyone else, they deserve to. The indictment is unanswerable, but is the conclusion inescapable? Not all have thought so.

• A number of Christian thinkers have opened the door a crack—sometimes, indeed, more than a crack—to find a place for "good pagans" in God's kingdom. The church's earliest defenders of the faith saw Greek philosophy as a God-taught preparation for the gospel among the Gentiles. They affirmed the salvation of Socrates, Plato, and their ilk through faith in the revelation they received of the preincarnate Word. This view still has its defenders.

• Many have urged the hope of universal salvation of infants through Christ's Cross—moving on from Augustine's and Dante's idea that unbaptized children who died would miss heaven but would be spared the pains of hell.

• The official Roman Catholic view was that there is no salvation outside the Roman communion and apart from its sacramental life. But the Council of Trent's statement that believers in the truth who, for whatever reason, cannot be baptized may yet be saved through "baptism of desire" (i.e., desire for baptism) has been further developed by Vatican II: "Those who, while guiltlessly ignorant of Christ's gospel and of his Church, sincerely seek God and are brought by the influence of grace to perform his will as known by the dictates of conscience, can achieve eternal salvation." The phrase "guiltlessly ignorant" points to ignorance that is invincible—that is, dominant and incurable, yet due wholly to conditioning, not to negligence or ill will or any intention, direct or remote, to disobey God. This notion was originally devised to explain how Protestants could be saved. But it is now used to affirm the possibility of salvation in any religion.

(One Protestant thinker hospitable to this idea was C. S. Lewis: In *The Last Battle*, Aslan says he views as offered to himself all service sincerely rendered to the false god Tash. Some Catholic theologians base their confidence of universal salvation on this line of thought.)

• Among Protestants, some Arminians hold that grace sufficient for salvation is given to everyone without exception—those who do not hear the gospel no less than those who do—so that everyone's salvation is in principle possible.

• Some Calvinists have guessed that God regenerates a certain number of unevangelized adults, bringing them to repentance and faith through general revelation alone.

• More recently, Karl Barth taught that in Christ crucified, all mankind was reprobated and condemned, and in Christ risen, all mankind is elected and justified. This has given a great fillip to explicit universalism—a conclusion that Barth himself seems to have avoided only by will power.

(Not all theologians, however, are as strong-willed as Barth. In much of today's Protestantism, belief in universal salvation, as the fruit and measure of Christ's redemptive victory, has become the standard view.)

Pressure points

The problem of the nonbeliever's destiny is acutely felt at present in the Western churches. There are at least three reasons for this:

Pastorally, pressure is felt because post-Christian pluralism and anti-Christian alternatives are always on our doorstep. We rub shoulders with people of other, ethnic faiths; with people who are "into" cults; with disillusioned ex-Christians; with hostile scientific humanists.

In the mainline churches we find a Pandora's boxful of mutated, not to say mutilated, Christianities: products of liberal randomness and radical reaction, of hermeneutical indiscipline, and sometimes, one fears, of sheer incompetence. Among evangelicals there remains something of a consensus on essentials, but evangelicals seem to be a quarter or less of the professing Christians in America and the Commonwealth, and outside evangelical circles one hears little more than what Eeyore called a "confused noise." How much of the faith of the Scriptures, we wonder, do those nurtured amid the confusion ever come to know?

Nor is this all. The public media, the national education system, and the literary establishments are resolutely secular, which means that men, women, and children—especially children—are being powerfully conditioned against biblical Christianity. What should we say of the nonbelief found among the victims of the ideological juggernaut? They did not create the secular ideology. It created them, molding them to its own sub-Christian shape.

To generous Christian hearts it seems nightmarish that unbelief resulting from the collapse of Christian culture round a person's head could ruin that person's soul.

The problem presses. What does the Bible say?

Theologically, pressure is felt because Christianity faces an up-surge of Islam and other great ethnic religions—all of which resent and reject Christianity's exlusive claim to be final truth from God for all mankind. As the world's population explodes, the percentage of our race that gives allegiance to Christianity keeps shrinking. This not only makes triumphalism impossible, but it also makes the universal significance of Jesus Christ seem problematical to many.

One response is the claim that Christ may be perceived, or posited, in existing ethnic faiths. In other words, these faiths should be understood as being already in essence what Christianity itself is. By the device of deft definition, this solves the problem of relating Christianity to other faiths. But it flies in the face of the fact that the closer one looks at ethnic religions, the more different from Christianity (both in ends proposed and in means to them) they are found to be. It leaves us with a new set of questions:

Should ordinary adherents of ethnic religions (who deny the Trinity, the Incarnation, the Atonement, and salvation by grace through faith whenever these tenets are put to them) be counted as "anonymous Christians"? Though they may be invincibly and therefore excusably ignorant, can we say that they are thus (because of their sincerity) being saved by the Christ whom, if they have heard of him at all, they reject? If so, why evangelize them? What is the point of asking anyone to change religions, if all religions are at bottom Christianity in disguise?

What does a Hindu or Muslim gain by becoming a Christian? Nothing, it seems, that he really did not have before. But shall we then discount the testimony of Hindu and Muslim converts that their conversion was a passage from death to life? Shall we conclude that the old liberal and theosophic notion of all religions climbing the same mountain and meeting at the top is true after all?

The questions press. Again we ask, what does the Bible say?

Strategically, pressure is felt because Protestantism is radically split about mission. *Mission* is shorthand for the task that the church is sent into the world to do in Christ's name, for love of God and neighbor. Two views clash as to what mission involves:

One view stands in line with the patristic, counter-Reformation Roman Catholic, and last-century Protestant missionary movements. It urges that the mandate is, first, to evangelize and plant churches; second, to relieve need at all levels, giving visibility and credibility to the good news of the Savior who makes us care for others; and third, to Christianize pagan cultures.

The view of some moderns, however, defines the mission as, first, to seek justice, peace, and prosperity in communities where these are lacking; second, to engage in dialogue with non-Christian religions in order to understand them and show them respect; and third, to nurture Christians and extend the church if time and circumstances permit—which, it is acknowledged, they may not.

The first view has now the Lausanne Covenant as its charter. The second reflects what was put forward by the WCC-sponsored conference at Bangkok on Salvation Today. Which set of priorities is right? What does the Bible say?

Ultimate optimism

Subordinating evangelism to sociopolitical concerns makes sense only if universalism is true. The universalist idea that all people will eventually be saved by grace is a comforting belief. It relieves anxiety about the destiny of pagans, atheists, devotees of non-Christian religions, victims of post-Christian secularity—the millions of adults who never hear the gospel and the millions of children who die before they can understand it. All sensitive Christians would like to embrace universalism; it would get us off a very painful hook. Let us see what can be said in its favor.

Modern universalism's basic idea is not that no one deserves to be damned, but that everyone will eventually be brought in humble gratitude to accept the acceptance with God that Christ's redemptive death won for them. Though hell is real, it will ultimately have no tenants.

Roman Catholic universalists hold that man's natural inclination toward goodness and God continues despite the Fall. It is sustained by universal grace and constitutes implicit faith—an openness to God through which Christ and his salvation will in due course, here or hereafter, be received even by Judas (a good test case by which to measure universalist reasoning).

Protestant universalists often say explicitly that those who leave this world in unbelief enter hell, but then exit, having been brought to their senses, encountered Christ, and embraced him while there. The essential claim is that hell does for the faithless what Roman Catholic purgatory does for believers; it fits them for the enjoyment of heaven.

Universalism is the ultimate optimism of grace, outstripping any form of mainstream Protestantism, Calvinist or Arminian. For universalists, hell is never the ultimate state. It is a stage on the journey home. Through postmortem encounter with Christ (a second chance for some, a first chance for others), God sovereignly calls and saves everyone out of what the New Testament calls "eternal punishment" and "eternal destruction" (Matt. 25:46; 2 Thess. 1:9, where *destruction* certainly means not annihilation, but a state of conscious ruin). No one is finally lost. Hell ends up empty.

Counterarguments

How is this view of hell's empty landscape supported? No biblical passage unambiguously asserts universal final salvation. Universalism is in fact a theological speculation that discounts the evident meaning of some New Testament passages in favor of what is claimed to be the overall thrust of New Testament thinking: that God's retributive justice toward men is always a disciplinary expression of redeeming love.

It would be nice to believe that; but Scripture nowhere suggests it when speaking of divine judgment, and the counterarguments seem overwhelmingly cogent:

1. Does not universalism ignore the constant biblical stress on the *decisiveness* and *finality* of this life's decisions for the determining of eternal destiny? Can this emphasis be evaded? Surely not.

2. Does not universalism condemn Christ himself, who warned men to flee hell at all costs, as having been either *incompetent* (ignorant that all were finally going to be saved) or *immoral* (knowing but concealing it, so as to bluff people into the kingdom through fear)? Can this dilemma be overcome? Surely not.

3. Does not the universalist idea of sovereign grace saving all nonbelievers after death raise new problems? If God's ability to bring all humans to faith eventually is posited, why would he not do it in this life in every case where the gospel is known? But if it is beyond God's power to convert all who know the gospel here, on what grounds can we be sure that he will be able to do it hereafter? Can any universalist's doctrine of God be made fully coherent? Surely not.

4. Does not the thoughtful Christian conscience reject universalism, just because one cannot apply it to oneself? "I dare not say to myself that if I forfeit the opportunity this life affords I shall ever have another; and therefore I dare not say so to another man," wrote James Denney. Is there any way around this? Surely not.

Universalism, therefore, will not work. This life's decisions must be deemed to be in every case decisive. And thus, proclaiming the gospel to our fallen, guilty, and hell-bent fellows must be the first service we owe them in light of their first and basic need. The proclamation must have the priority that the older, the historic catholic, mission strategy gave it.

"I am under obligation both to Greeks and to barbarians ... to preach the gospel," wrote Paul. "For 'every one who calls upon the name of the Lord will be saved.' But how are men to call upon him ... of whom they have never heard? ... Faith comes from what is heard, and what is heard comes by the preaching of Christ" (Rom. 1:14–15, 10:13–14, 17, citing Joel 2:32).

Light for all

But could God, in particular cases, work with and through the light of general revelation—light that comes to every human being—to evoke repentance and faith, and thus to bring about the salvation of some to whom no verbal message about God forgiving sins has ever come?

The question is prompted by Peter's statement: "In every nation anyone who fears him and does right is acceptable" (Acts 10:35). It is supported by Paul's assertion: "[God] did not leave himself without witness" (14:17). Add to that his strong declaration of general revelation from God to all mankind in Romans 1:18–2:16. Consider the acknowledgment and worship of Israel's God by Melchizedek, Jethro, Job, Abimelech, Baalam, Naaman, the sailors in Jonah's boat, Cyrus, and Nebuchadnezzar. Compare John's description of the preincarnate Word as "the true light that enlightens every man" (John 1:9; cf. v. 4) with his analysis of the sinner's judgment as flight from the light, while "he who does what is true comes to the light" (3:19–21). That God will judge us all according to what we have done with the light we were given, and that that is supremely just on his part, I take for granted.

In *Christianity and World Religions*, Sir Norman Anderson states the question as it relates to non-Christian worshipers: "Might it not be true of the follower of some other religion that the God of all mercy had worked in his heart by his Spirit, bringing him in some measure to realize his sin and need for forgiveness, and enabling him, in his twilight as it were, to throw himself on God's mercy?"

The answer seems to be yes, it might be true, as it may well have been true for at least some of the Old Testament characters. If ever it is true, such worshipers will learn in heaven that they were saved by Christ's death and that their hearts were renewed by the Holy Spirit, and they will join the glorified church in endless praise of the sovereign grace of God. Christians since the second century have hoped so, and perhaps Socrates and Plato are in this happy state even now—who knows?

But we have no warrant to expect that God will act thus in any single case where the gospel is not known or understood. Therefore our missionary obligation is not one whit diminished by our entertaining this possibility. Nor will this idea make the anti-Christian thrust of non-Christian religions seem any less than it did before.

If we are wise, we shall not spend much time mulling over this notion. Our job, after all, is to spread the gospel, not to guess what might happen to those to whom it never comes. Dealing with them is God's business: he is just and also merciful, and when we learn, as one day we shall, how he has treated them we shall have no cause to complain. Meantime, let us keep before our minds mankind's universal need of forgiveness and new birth, and the graciousness of the "whosoever will" invitations of the gospel. And let us redouble our efforts to make known the Christ who saves to the uttermost all who come to God by him.

What Will Happen to Those Who Will Not Repent?

Roger Nicole

Part of the appeal of universalism is its apparent scriptural support. Because of this, the concept of universal salvation has a ring of orthodoxy. Consider the manner in which universalists appeal to Scripture:

1. They build their case on Scriptures that are construed to teach a universal saving will of God (Ezek. 18:23, 32; John 3:16–17; 1 Tim. 2:4; 2 Pet. 3:9).

2. They use Scriptures that suggest the death of Christ had a

universal intent articulated by the words *world, all, everyone,* and *whoever.*

3. They quote passages that represent the final state as one of total subservience to God: "the renewal of all things" (Matt. 19:28; cf. Acts 3:21); "all flesh shall see the salvation of God" (Isa. 40:5; 52:10; 62:2; Luke 3:6); "to bring all things on heaven and earth together under one head, even Christ" (Eph. 1:10; cf. Col. 1:20); "that . . . every knee should bow . . . and every tongue confess . . ." (Phil. 2:10–11); "He has put everything under his feet" (1 Cor. 15:27–28); ". . . that God may be all in all" (1 Cor. 15:28; all Scripture quotations taken from the NIV).

4. They quote passages where death is represented as subdued in the *eschaton* (1 Cor. 15:26; Rev. 20:14).

These Scriptures, considered in isolation, constitute a fairly strong case, especially when combined with a deep yearning in our hearts for an ultimate abolishment of evil. We do not, however, have the luxury of dealing with any Scripture in isolation. Specifically, we must note the expressions used to denote the fate of the impenitent:

Separation from God. Death and hell can be described as separation from God for whose service we were made, and outside of whom there is nothing but futility and hopeless frustration. In referring to the unrepentant, Jesus said, "Depart from me" (Matt. 25:41). Numerous references in the New Testament support the idea that those who reject Christ are "shut out of the presence of the Lord and from the majesty of his power" (2 Thess. 1:9).

Destruction and death. This type of language does not so much imply cessation of existence as a complete deprivation of some element essential to normal and fruitful existence. This total waste is perhaps the basis for the use of the word *gehenna,* the name of the Jerusalem dump where rubbish was burned.

Fire. Beneficial to humanity when kept under control, fire may nonetheless develop into a terrible scourge. This is perhaps the most common figurative language of Scripture to represent the torment of the damned, with references to consuming fire, everlasting burning, the lake of fire, and burning sulphur being most familiar.

From the frequency of this language, some have inferred that physical fire burns the bodies of the reprobates. While this is not strictly impossible, it appears unlikely since physical fire appears in conflict with other scriptural descriptions of hell (outer darkness, bottomless pit). Also, it appears ill suited to resurrection bodies that might seem impervious to it. The spiritual fire, however, that consumes and sears the soul, is perhaps more terrifying and excruciating than physical burning.

Darkness (Matt. 8:12; 22:13; 25:30; Jude 6, 13). Since God is light and the source of light, it is not surprising that separation from him implies darkness forever.

The worm that will not die (Isa. 66:24; Mark 9:48). This may well refer to the gnawing pains eating away at the vitals of the soul.

Trouble, distress, torment, agony. These terms emphasize the conscious suffering of the damned, as does the word *punishment* (*kolasis*) used by Jesus (Matt. 25:46), as well as the passages where our Lord speaks of weeping, wailing, or gnashing of teeth (Matt. 8:12; 13:42, 50). The implication of consciousness is reinforced in Revelation 20:10, where we read of being "tormented day and night for ever and ever."

Shame and everlasting contempt. This emphasizes the disgrace experienced by the lost who will now see their rebellion in its true light (Dan. 12:2; Isa. 66:24).

Everlasting chains and *gloomy dungeons.* Punishment for sin includes the loss of the potential to do as one pleases. Contrary to what many imagine, it is the people of God who enjoy glorious liberty in obedience to God, while the sinner is detained in shameful slavery. Heaven and hell are the definitive expression of this truth.

Futility. This concept surfaces in Scripture in relation to the life that is shipwrecked away from God. "Meaningless, utterly meaningless," says the teacher, "a chasing after the wind" (Eccles. 1:2, 14). "What good is it for a man to gain the whole world, yet forfeit his soul?" (Mark 8:36; Luke 9:25).

The wrath of God. A final form of biblical language must be noted in the many places relating to the damned (John 3:36; Rom. 2:5, 8; Eph. 2:3; Heb. 10:27). This expression appears more than 600 times in Scripture. The word *propitiation* bears emphatic witness to God's fundamental displeasure at the sight of sin.

Though some Scripture appeals to a universalistic understanding of salvation, in the final analysis the universalist must face the more consistent scriptural treatment of a final judgment to which all humankind is summoned and which issues into a *bifurcation of destiny*.

The universalist faces further difficulties with passages relating to the unpardonable sin, the great chasm between the rich man and Lazarus over which no one could cross, Jesus' statement "Where I go, you cannot come," and particularly with his remark about Judas: "It would be better for him if he had not been born." How could someone who is ultimately going to be saved be called "the son of perdition"? How can a universalist fairly deal with the many Scriptures that show that life's decisions have everlasting and irrevocable consequences in the life to come?

Endless punishment and God's love

Some approach universalism from the perspective of punishment. They argue that the endlessness of punishment is unjust because the sanction is not proportionate with the fault. But this disregards the fact that time is not a primary factor: a fault of a brief moment may well have lifelong consequences. The universalist does not sufficiently weigh the gravity of the offense in rejecting God. Furthermore, the reprobates in hell are not in a penitential mood; they continue in their senseless rebellion. In a sense, they would be worse off being exposed in all their ugliness to the full light of the presence of God than in groveling in their darkness away from him (John 3:20).

To this, however, the universalists object on the basis of God's love. It is inconsistent with this love, they urge, to imagine that God upholds the existence of a great many rational beings, angelic and human, just to wreak vengeance upon them. In pressing this argument, the tendency is present to minimize the importance of sin. All these arguments grounded in an appeal to God's love ignore his honor and righteousness. Love that is not accompanied by righteousness is merely sentimental weakness and has no connection with a scriptural understanding of God's love. Here the concerns of holiness are so important that God was willing to give his only Son as a substitute "so as to be just and the one who justifies the man who has faith in Jesus" (Rom. 3:26). It is the fearful reality and the inexpressible sadness of perdition that account for the sacrifice on the cross. Where these are toned down there is inevitably an erosion of the significance of Christ's work. In the Universalist denomination, the deity of Christ was soon jettisoned after his atoning sacrifice was downplayed.

We must remember that the very person who revealed most stunningly God's love, our Lord Jesus Christ, is also the one who spoke most frequently and in the most frightening words of the tragedy of the lost. It is dangerous to be more generous than God has revealed himself to be!

If the plight of the unbelievers is what the Bible reveals it to be, it is not an act of love to hide their fate from them. To do so further blinds them to the remedy God provided. If a person is struck with a deadly disease for which there is a known cure, it is neither wise nor loving to try and convince him that nothing is wrong.

Chapter 10

WHAT WILL HEAVEN BE LIKE?

Peter Kreeft

Asking questions about Heaven may seem like asking questions about Katmandu, Kuala Lumpur, or some other exotic place you are unlikely to see firsthand—an occasion for speculation. But writing about Heaven is not really like writing about faraway places with strange-sounding names, for writing about Heaven is really writing about God. A creation reflects a Creator and the laws of a kingdom, the ideals of the King. So asking whether we will have sex in Heaven or whether our pets will be there is really asking what kind of God we serve and what his best intentions are for our eternity.

Philosopher Peter Kreeft agreed to write this chapter because CHRISTIANITY TODAY still capitalized Heaven (which it usually doesn't) "as if it were a real place like Boston" (which it is) "rather than a wispy abstraction like 'wellness.'" In this essay, Kreeft addresses (often whimsically) 35 frequently asked questions about Heaven (and here CHRISTIANITY TODAY capitalizes Heaven).

I n this brief chapter I would like to attempt the impossible: to answer the 35 most frequently asked questions about Heaven. Obviously, it would take more than an article, more than a lifetime, and more than human wisdom to answer any one of these questions adequately. But "fools rush in where angels fear to tread." More seriously, sometimes a taste can whet the appetite for more complete consumption later on, and perhaps these samples will at least suggest ways to think about the subject.

1. *How do we know anything about Heaven, anyway?* If we had no "inside information," we could only speculate. Fortunately, we have some solid data to build on: divine revelation. I think God wants us to use our reason and also our imagination (for why should we neglect any God-given faculty) to explore the treasure of tantalizing hints in Scripture. To be indifferent to it is to be like the unprofitable servant who hid his master's talent in the ground. In having this data, we are in a position very different from that of the unbeliever (or rather, the difference lies in our *believing* the data, for the whole human race *has* it; it is public). We are like the sighted compared to the blind, who can only speculate about things visible. We can do more than speculate about things invisible.

"What do you know about Heaven, anyway? Have you ever been there?" We can answer this challenge: "No, but I have a very good Friend who has. He came here and told us about it and showed it to us. He is the Way, the Truth, and the Life."

2. *Why won't we be bored in Heaven?* I suspect this question subconsciously bothers most of us more than we like to admit. I can remember having something of a crisis of faith as a child: I thought I didn't want to go to Heaven since the popular pictures of it seemed pretty boring to me. Freud, who occasionally comes up with nuggets of wisdom sandwiched between mountains of nonsense, says that everyone needs two things to make life worth living: love and work. The two are really one, for love is a work and work is a love. Love is a work, for it is something you do, not something you just feel or fall into. And work must be a love, for if not, it is threatening and boring. What love-work will we do in Heaven, then?

We will complete the very love-works we are meant to do on Earth. There are only six things that never get boring on Earth, six things that never come to an end: knowing and loving yourself, your neighbor, and God. Since persons are subjects and not objects, they are not exhaustible; they are like magic cows that give fresh milk forever. The two great commandments that are our job description for life, in both this world and the next, express this plan: We must love God wholly and we must love our neighbor as ourself. And in order to love we must know, get to know, as endlessly as we love endlessly. This never gets boring, even on Earth: getting to know and love more and more someone we already know and love. It is our clue and our preparation for our eternal destiny of infinite fascination.

3. *Will we recognize our loved ones in Heaven?* George Macdonald answers this question with a counterquestion: "Will we be greater fools there than here?" Of course we will know our loved ones. This is a divinely designed, essential part of our joy. We are not designed to be solitary mystics, lovers of God alone, but to be, like God himself, lovers of men and women as well.

Just as Jesus on Earth loved each person differently and specially—he did not love John as he loved Peter, because John was not Peter—so we are designed to love people specially. There is no reason why this specialness should be removed, rather than added to, in eternity. Our family and special friends will always be our family and special friends. In this life a child begins to learn to love by loving mother, then father, then siblings, then pets. The concentric circles of love are then gradually expanded, but the beginning lessons are never abandoned. There is no reason to think God rips up this plan after death.

4. *How can I be happy in Heaven if someone I loved deeply on Earth doesn't make it to Heaven?* This brings up all sorts of other questions about emotions, relationships, and suffering in Heaven. These will be dealt with shortly, but the simplest and most important answer to this question for now is this: If there is someone you love and identify with so deeply that you cannot imagine being happy in eternity without him or her, and that someone seems now to be in peril of being unsaved, then use the relationship that God's providence has ordained for you. Tell God that he *has* to arrange for this person's salvation as he has arranged for yours, because this person is a real part of you, and for you as a whole to be saved, this person has to come along, just as your own body and emotions have to come along. It need not be a "wheedling" or "blackmail" prayer; it can be

a simple presentation of the facts, like Mary's "They have no more wine." Let God do his thing: it is always more loving, more gracious, and more effective than our thing, more than we can ever imagine or desire. Trust him to use your earthly love as a channel, supernatural and/or natural, of grace and salvation for your friend. Your very question, your very problem, is the clue to its answer. God put that burden on your heart for a reason: for you to fulfill.

5. *Can suicides be saved?* Simply, yes. Most people who commit suicide are not in full control of their reason and thus are not fully responsible. Suicide is a dreadful mistake, of course, and a terrible sin. But only *unrepented* sin locks Heaven's door, and sometimes sins are repented of at the same time they are committed, or immediately afterward. The deeper part of a suicide's soul and will may believe and hope in and love God even while the surface part drives him to despair. Or repentance may come in an instant between the act and its result, death, or even *at* the moment of death. We do not know. Only God sees and judges hearts, not just acts, and God will use every possible means to save us. Perhaps many of those means are unknown and unsuspected by us. No one dare limit the mercy, the cleverness, or the power of God.

But our very uncertainty should send us running from this horribly dangerous sin in holy terror. Those who commit suicide do not automatically ensure their damnation, but they certainly risk their salvation.

6. *Will we have emotions in Heaven?* This question prompts a series of questions of the form: Will we have the following earthly thing in Heaven? I believe the answer to all such questions is this: Yes, but not in the present form. Nothing is simply continued, and nothing is simply lost forever; everything is transformed, as it is at birth.

We can know very little about this transformation, of course, and our answers must be largely disciplined guesswork. But I strongly suspect that we will have emotions in Heaven, for they are part of God's design for our humanity, and not only a result of the Fall. But our emotions will not drive us or control us. They will be no less passionate, but they will be less passive. Thomas Aquinas opines that sexual enjoyment was greater, not less, before the Fall (since sin always harms, never helps, every good thing), and Augustine opines that in Heaven the joy that we receive from God in our souls will "overflow" into our resurrection bodies in a "voluptuous torrent" of pleasure.

7. *If we have emotions in Heaven, why won't we be sad about those we loved who are in hell?* We know there is no sadness in Heaven: God "will wipe away every tear from their eyes" (Rev. 7:17). I think we will not be sad about the damned for the same reason God is not. According to the Sermon on the Mount, he will say to them, "I never knew you" (Matt. 7:23). God will wipe our memories clean. This is not falsehood or ignorance, but truth, for in a sense, the damned no longer *are*—that is, they no longer are in the most real place of all, Heaven. They no longer *count*. They are like ashes, not like wood. They once were fully human, fully alive, real men and women. But hell is a place not of eternal *life* but of eternal *death*. We do not love or weep over ashes; we only love or weep over the thing that existed before it was burnt. In Heaven, however, we will not live in the past—we will have no regrets; nor will we live in the future—we will have no fears; but like God, we will live in the eternal present. Our heavenly emotions will be appropriate to present reality, not past reality.

8. *Does this mean hell is unreal?* Certainly not. Jesus is very clear about the reality of hell. But he is also clear that it is death, not life, for the soul. In Greek philosophy, souls cannot die. In Christianity, they can—in hell. Is this annihilation? No, it is death. Annihilation is the opposite of creation; death is the opposite of life.

9. *What happens in hell?* Nothing.

10. *What happens in Heaven?* Everything.

11. *Can the blessed in Heaven see us now?* Let me put it this way: Is there any compelling reason why they shouldn't? Would their perfection be threatened thereby? Can Heaven be Heaven only by being quarantined and having the blinds drawn? It is reasonable to interpret the "cloud of witnesses" in Hebrews 12:1 not only as witnesses to their faith during their own lifetimes but as witnesses to us, now; not just as the dead "witness *to*" the living by *our* memory of them but as the living *witness* the living by *their* living consciousness. Is there anything wrong with your love of your family? Will there be anything wrong with it in Heaven? Will there be anything wrong with your desire to see how they fare on Earth? I

see no compelling reason to answer no.

12. *Will we know everything in Heaven?* I think not. Only God is omniscient. We will never stop learning, but we will never come to the end, either. Only God can endure knowing everything without being bored.

13. *Will we all be equal in Heaven?* We will be as we are now: equal in worth and dignity, equal in being loved by God. But will we be equal in the sense of the same? God forbid! One of the chief pleasures of this life, as of the next, is the mutual sharing of different excellences, the pleasure of looking up to someone who is better than we are at something and learning from him or her. The resentment expressed in saying, "I'm just as good as you are" is hellish, not heavenly. (By the way, that is one sentence that always means the opposite of what it says. No one who says it believes it.)

14. *Do differences include sexual differences? Is there sex in Heaven?* Of course. Sex is part of our divinely designed humanity. It is transformed, not removed, in Heaven. We will be "like the angels" in "neither marrying nor being given in marriage," according to Christ's answer to the Sadducees (Matt. 22:30), but not in being neutered. Sex is first of all something we *are*, not something we *do*. I do not think we will be "doing" copulation in Heaven, but we will be busy *being* ourselves, and that includes being men and women, not genderless geldings. *Vive la différence!*

15. *What kind of bodies will we have in Heaven?* Gnostics of all kinds (Platonists, Buddhists, Hindus, Spiritualists, Manichaeans) say we will become pure spirits, angels, for they do not know the dogma of Creation. Pagans and Muslims say we will have earthly bodies and harems or happy hunting grounds. Christians say we will have transformed bodies, but real, physical bodies, as Christ had after his resurrection. His body could be touched and could eat. Yet it could come and go as he pleased, with neither walls nor distance as an obstacle. It was the same body he had before he died, and it was recognized as such by his friends. Yet it was so different that at first they did *not* recognize him. I think our new resurrection body will be related to the body we have now in the same way that our current body is related to the body we had in our mothers' wombs. If a fetus saw a picture of itself at the age of twenty, it would at first not recognize itself, so unforeseen and surprisingly new would it be. Yet

it is the same self, even the same body, now grown radically more mature.

16. *What of injuries and deformities? Will they all be removed in the resurrection body?* I think not. Christ still had his wounds. But they were badges of glory, not suffering and sadness. I think everything—in the body, in the soul, and in the person's world—that was offered to God and taken up into the eternal kingdom will be preserved and transformed and glorified in Heaven: but everything that was not—everything that was not the work of God or of the sanctified soul but was of the world, the flesh, or the devil—will be left outside Heaven's gate. The martyrs' wounds will glow like gold, but the amputee's limb will be restored, and so will the brain-damaged person's intelligence. God's justice and mercy are perfect, and so is his style.

17. *Will there be nature in Heaven?* Scripture tells us there will be "a new heaven [that is, sky] and a new earth" (Rev. 21:1). If we have a new body, we need a new Earth: bodies are not for drifting in empty space. And if a world, why a dead world, like the moon, rather than a world brimming with life, like this Earth? I think we will have a much *more* intimate relationship with nature than we do now, not less. I think the images of the nature mystics and pantheist poets are almost right, but as prophecy: In the heavenly future we will get inside the secret of life that we now stare at as outsiders. C. S. Lewis suggests, in his great sermon "The Weight of Glory," that the reason we have peopled the Earth with gods and goddesses is so that these projections of ours can do what we long to do but cannot do, or at least cannot do yet: touch the inner secret of the beauty we see in nature. "But all the leaves of the New Testament are rustling with the rumor that it will not always be so. Some day, God willing, we will get *in*."

18. *Will we be able to perform magic and miracles?* I think so. Powers that are now largely denied us, for our own safety, will be restored to us when we have learned to use them well. When our souls follow the will of God like orchestra players follow the baton of their conductor, then we will play in harmony. But just imagine what havoc God would allow if he gave us preternatural powers over nature in our fallen condition!

19. *Will there be animals in Heaven? Will my dead cat be there?* The

simplest answer I know to this question, so frequently asked by children, is: Why not? Children's questions are usually the best ones, and we should beware treating them with any less seriousness than their askers have in asking them. Right now, pets, like everything else in this world, can mediate God's love and goodness to us and train us for our union with him, *or* they can distract us from him. In Heaven, everything mediates and nothing distracts.

20. *Will we eat in Heaven?* We will have bodies, so we will be *able* to eat, as Christ did after the resurrection. But I think we will not *have* to eat. The resurrection body will live off the soul and the soul off God. As we are now, our bodies are dependent on what is less than they are, subsidies from nature; and our souls are dependent on what is less than they are, our bodies (if our brains are damaged, we cannot think well). This situation of being hostage to our inferiors must be reversed. Perhaps the matter of which the resurrection body will be composed will not have separate atoms and molecules (and so will be indestructible). Perhaps our bodies will not have separate organs and systems, but the body as a whole, or the whole soul in the whole body, will perform all of its operations. But of course this is pure speculation.

21. *Will our bodies be clothed in Heaven?* Those who claim to have caught some glimpse of people in Heaven, whether in a vision or in a near-death experience, usually say that the people in Heaven are clothed, but differently than we are. The clothing is not artificial and concealing, but natural and revealing. Clothing came after the Fall, to conceal what was shameful only because it was fallen. Once redemption is complete and the Fall wholly reversed, nothing is shameful. Clothes will then be a pure glory, not half glory and half shame, as they now are. Perhaps they will seem to grow out of the resurrection body itself rather than be put on from outside. The issue is more important than it seems, because clothing symbolizes the whole world and our relationship with our world. We take parts of our world unto ourselves as clothes and make them intimate parts of our lives. In Heaven we will clothe ourselves with the new heavens and the new earth, like the "woman clothed with the sun" in Revelation 12:1.

22. *Will there be music in Heaven?* Indeed. Even now, great music seems like an echo from Eden, a souvenir, a memory from Paradise—

something not merely pleasant but profoundly meaningful in an ungraspable, unformulatable way, a high and holy mystery. Once again I refer (only as a clue) to numerous visionaries who have said they heard music in Heaven, but of such a different quality from earthly music that it was incomparable—like comparing a toddler's banging on a toy xylophone with a symphony orchestra.

Music, according to widespread tradition, was the first language, the language God spoke to create the universe. I strongly suspect there is more to this than we think. We usually think of music as ornamented poetry and of poetry as ornamented prose. But God is not prosaic. I think prose is fallen poetry and poetry fallen music. In the beginning was the "music of the spheres," and so it will be in the end.

23. *Will Heaven be big?* Yes, but with a different kind of bigness. Now, space contains us, confines us, defines us. But we can transform *space* into *place* by humanizing it, spiritualizing it. A house becomes a home, a space becomes a place, by our living in it. Heaven will be both as intimate and as unconfining as our spirits want. No one will think it too small or too large. In a sense, it will be in us rather than we in it—not in the sense that it will be subjective, but in the sense in which stage settings and props are in a play, or part of a play, rather than the play being in or part of the setting.

24. *Is Heaven in this universe?* No. If it were, you could get there by rocket ship. It is another dimension, not another world. Yet, in a sense, it is continuous with this world, somewhat as this one is continuous with the world of the womb. From the viewpoint of an unborn child, this world is distant and outside the womb; but from the viewpoint of a born person, the womb is in the world, and the unborn child is already in the world—the child just doesn't see this until after birth. I suspect that from the viewpoint of Heaven we will truly say that Earth was part of Heaven, Heaven's womb. But you cannot get there by rocket, only by faith and death, just as the fetus cannot get into the world outside the womb except by birth.

25. *Will there be time in Heaven?* Eternity does not mean simply endless time; that would be boring. Nor does it mean something strictly timeless; that would be inhuman. Time is part of our consciousness, and God does not tear up his plan for us; rather, he fulfills and transforms it. I think eternity will include all time, as the

dying see their whole life pass before them in perfect temporal order, not confusion, yet instantaneously—somewhat as you can do now when you call to mind a story you have read and know well. When you say "David Copperfield," you mean all the Davids, in order, but you see them all at once, from the young David to the old David, because, having finished the story, you are outside it. You are "after death" regarding David. One day you will be "after death" regarding yourself. Time now confines us. There is never enough of it. I think heavenly time will be like heavenly space: fully humanized and subject to the soul. Even now there are two kinds of time, as there are two kinds of space (space and place): *chronos*, or chronological time, material time, and *kairos*, or lived time, human time, time *for* some purpose measured by mind and will. Now, *kairos* is contained and constrained by *chronos*; there is seldom enough time to do justice to anything. In heaven this inside-out situation will be reversed, and chronological time will be contained and mastered by *kairos*, somewhat as even now playwrights and novelists master the time in their stories.

Our dissatisfaction with time, by the way, is a powerful piece of evidence that we are made for eternity. There is nothing more natural and all-pervasive in this world than time. Not only our bodies but our souls as well are immersed in time. Yet we complain about it. C. S. Lewis asks, "Do fish complain of the sea for being wet? Or if they did, would that fact not strongly suggest that they had not been, or were not destined always to be, aquatic creatures?" We long to step out of the sea of time onto the land of eternity, even though we do not really understand what eternity is!

26. *What age will we be in Heaven?* Medieval philosophers usually thought we would all be 33, the ideal age, the age of maturity, as of Christ's earthly maturity. I take it this is symbolically accurate: we will all be fully mature. Infants who die prematurely will be given, by God (perhaps through the mediation of their own parents!), all the maturing they missed on Earth.

Geneticists say that the aging process is not inevitable; that a live organism could theoretically be immortal, never age, never die. Cancer cells do not die unless they are killed or their host dies. The aging and dying process began at a certain time in our history, after the Fall. God did not make death, but he unmakes it. In Heaven no one will be old. Yet in a sense everyone will be both old and young, as a reflection of the God who is the Alpha and Omega, oldest and youngest, "beauty ancient yet ever new." Even now we sometimes see the wisdom of old age in the musing face of a baby or the eternal freshness of youth in the twinkling eyes of the very old. These are hints of Heaven.

27. *What language will we speak in Heaven?* My ancestors stoutly maintained that it would be Dutch, of course. A rabbi I know has told me it will be Hebrew; every baby, he said, still remembers the language that will be restored in Heaven, the language of Eden, as evidenced by the fact that a child's first word is often *abba* ("Father" or "Daddy" in Hebrew). It will be none of the languages that now divide us, which began at Babel. Babel and its babble will be reversed. This was foreshadowed at Pentecost, where distinctive languages were preserved, not muddled, yet each person understood everyone else. Perhaps there will be as many languages as there are individuals, and yet at the same time only one. What is sure is that there will be no misunderstanding. Language, like clothing, now both reveals and conceals, unveils and veils meaning. In Heaven, language, like clothing, will only reveal.

28. *Will there be privacy in Heaven?* I think not. No one will want to hold anything back, for no one will be ashamed or afraid of being misunderstood or unloved. Privacy is like clothes and like laws: necessary only because we are fallen. When sin is gone, all hiding will be gone.

Certainly there will be no private property, no "this is mine, not yours." Communism, like nudism and anarchism, dimly sees something heavenly, but by insisting on enacting it now, by human force, it turns the heavenly into the hellish, as when adult powers are given to infants.

29. *Will we be free in Heaven? If so, will we be free to sin? If so, won't anyone ever exercise that freedom?* "Freedom to sin" is a contradiction in terms, like "freedom to be enslaved." Free choice is only the *means* to true freedom, "the freedom of the sons of God," liberty.

In heaven we will not sin because we will not want to. We will freely choose never to sin, just as now great mathematicians do not make elementary mistakes, though they have the power to do so. In Heaven we will see the attractiveness of goodness and of God so clearly, and the ugliness and stupidity of sin so clearly, that there will be no possible motive to sin. Now, we are enslaved by ignorance. Every sin comes from ignorance, for we sin only because we see sin as somehow attractive, which it is not, and goodness as somehow lacking in attraction. This is an ignorance that we are responsible for, but it *is* ignorance, and without that ignorance we would not sin. In Heaven, in the "beatific vision" of God, overwhelmed and filled with the total joy of goodness, baptized with goodness as a sunken ship is filled with water, no one could possibly ever want to turn from this perceived glory. Now, "we walk by faith, not by sight"(2 Cor. 5:7). Heavenly sight will not remove our freedom. Ask the blind whether sight would remove their freedom.

30. *Isn't concern about Heaven escapist?* I answer the question with another question, from C. S. Lewis: Who talks the most against "escapism"? Jailers. Is it escapist for a baby to wonder about life outside the womb? Is it escapist for someone on a long ocean voyage to wonder about landfall? Is it escapist for the seed to dream of the flower? It is escapist if, and only if, Heaven is a lie. Those who call Heaven "escapism" are presupposing atheism.

31. *But doesn't concern for Heaven detract from concern for Earth?* No, just the opposite. Does a pregnant woman's concern for her baby's future detract from concern for her baby's present? If she believes her baby will be born dead, she will cease to take care of it, and if we believe that this life ends with a cosmic abortion, we will cease to take much care of it. But if we believe that this life is the preparation for eternity, then everything makes an eternal difference. The early roads that led to California were well cared for; the ones that led nowhere were abandoned. If Earth is the road to Heaven, we will care for it. If it leads nowhere, we will not. Historically, it is those who have believed most strongly in Heaven who have made the greatest difference to Earth, beginning with Christ himself.

32. *How intimate is the connection between Heaven and Earth? Does Heaven begin now?* The joy of Heaven does, because Christ *is* our joy, who tells us "I am with you always, even to the end of the world" (Matt. 28:20, Phillips). We do not now fully appreciate that joy, but it is here, because the very life of Heaven, the very life that flows from the Vine into the branches, is here. If it is not here in us

now, it will not be there in us then. If Heaven is not in us now, we will not be in Heaven forever. For Heaven is where God is. God determines where Heaven is; Heaven does not determine where God is. God contains Heaven; Heaven does not contain God. If God is in our souls now by faith, then the very life of Heaven is here in us now, in seed form. That is what Jesus came to preach about and to give, the focus of all his sermons: "the kingdom of Heaven." It is the "pearl of great price," the thing for which the whole world is far too small a price to pay. And it is free.

33. *How do you get to Heaven?* This is the most important question anyone can ask. The answer has already been given: It is free. "Let him who is thirsty come, let him who desires take the water of life without price" (Rev. 22:17). Faith is the act of taking.

It sounds crazy, too good to be true. But it makes perfect sense. For God is love. Love gives gifts, gives itself. God gives himself, his own life, membership in his family. We are made "partakers of the divine nature" (2 Peter 1:4). For God is pure love, and pure love has no admixture of stinginess in it.

34. *Is Jesus the only way? (Or can good pagans, Hindus, et cetera get to Heaven too?)* The first part of the question is clear, and the answer is clear: Unless Jesus is the victim of grandiose self-delusion or deliberate, blasphemous lying, he is the only way, for he says exactly that (John 14:6). But the second part of the question is not clear. People who have never heard of Christ, and thus have neither consciously accepted him nor consciously rejected him, must also get to Heaven through Christ, for there is no other way. That much is clear from Christ's own words. But it is not clear what is going on in the unconscious depths of the souls of such people. Only God knows. Perhaps they know and love him in the obscure form of a deep, unconscious desire and love.

The game of heavenly population statistics is one that Christ discouraged his disciples from playing. When they asked him, "Are many saved?" he answered neither yes nor no but said, "Strive to enter in" (Luke 13:24). In other words, mind your own business, your own salvation, rather than speculating about others and statistics. God has not told us the answer to this question, for his own good reasons, just as he has not told us when the world will end, another question about which we love to speculate. I think that in both cases we can see the wisdom of not telling us. If we knew when the world would end, we would not be ready at all times for the thief who comes in the night, unexpectedly. If we knew that most were not saved, we would tend to despair; if we knew that most were saved, we would tend to presumption.

What we do know is that Christ the Savior is not only a 33-year-old, 6-foot-high Jewish man, but also the eternal God, the Logos that enlightens every individual (John 1:9). Thus everyone has a fair chance to accept him or reject him, whether implicitly (for all light of truth and goodness is from him) or explicitly. We are not saved by how explicit our knowledge is; we are saved by him. Faith is the glue that holds him fast (or, more accurately, the glue by which he holds us fast, for faith is also his gift).

This is a traditional, mainline Christian position, from the time of Justin Martyr and Clement of Alexandria to the time of C. S. Lewis. It is halfway between the liberal view that one can be saved in other ways than Christ (for example, by good intentions) and the frequent fundamentalist view that it takes an *explicit* knowledge of Christ to be saved.

The middle view does not detract from the infinite seriousness of missionary work, as the liberal view does. For if we do not know how many children will fall through a hole in the ice and drown, we feel just as much urgency in shouting warnings (and in putting our words into action) as we would if we knew exactly who would die and who would not.

35. *How do you think all these questions and answers will look to you in Heaven?* I think they will look very much like Michelangelo's first lump of clay—worked on at the age of two—looked to him after he had sculpted the *Pietà*. I think we will see these childish babblings about "what no eye has seen, nor ear heard, nor the heart of man conceived" (1 Cor. 1:9) as we will see everything else in our present lives: suffused with the light and love of God. And so we will cherish these childish toys, even as we laugh at them. Seeing and loving God in all good things, including our own, is what we were made for, and what we will be doing forever without boredom. We had better get some practice now.

In the light of Heaven, everything we do and everything we experience takes on two new meanings. On the one hand, everything becomes infinitely more important, more serious, more weighted with glory than before. If we are practicing only for a casual pastime, our practice is not terribly important, but if we are practicing for the world championship, it is. On the other hand, Heaven makes everything earthly seem light and trivial by comparison. Saint Theresa says that the most horrible, suffering-filled life on Earth, looked at from Heaven, will seem no more than a night in an inconvenient hotel. Saints and martyrs know the value of this life and this world; they love it because God loves it. But they lightly give it all up for Heaven. Heavenly light gives us not only "an eternal *weight* of glory," but at the same time a lightsome spirit, as in the Cavalier poet:

Man, please Thy maker and be merry,
And for this world give not a cherry.

ABOUT THE AUTHORS

Colin Brown *is professor of systematic theology and associate dean and director of the Center for Advanced Theological Studies at Fuller Theological Seminary, Pasadena, California. He is a graduate of the Universities of Liverpool, London, Nottingham, and Bristol, where he obtained his doctorate for work on the study of Jesus. He has discussed the subject of miracles in his award-winning book,* Miracles and the Critical Mind *(Eerdmans, 1984) and his paperback,* That You May Believe: Miracles and Faith—Then and Now *(Eerdmans, 1985). The article included in this volume draws on material discussed more fully in* That You May Believe, *and is used here by kind permission of the publishers.*

Rodney Clapp *is a senior writer for* CHRISTIANITY TODAY. *He is a graduate of Oklahoma State University and the Wheaton Graduate School of Communications. He is currently studying ethics at Bethany Theological Seminary, Oakbrook, Illinois. Clapp is coauthor with Robert Webber of* People of the Truth: The Power of the Worshiping Community in the Modern World *(Harper & Row, 1988).*

Bonnidell Clouse *is professor of educational and school psychology at Indiana State University, Terre Haute, Indiana. She is a graduate of Wheaton College, Boston University, and Indiana University, from which she earned her Ph.D. She is a contributing editor to the* Journal of Psychology and Theology, *and her article from that journal, "The Teachings of Jesus and Piaget's Concept of Mature Moral Judgment," has been included in* Psychology and Christianity: Integrative Readings *(Abingdon, 1981). She is the author of* Moral Development: Perspectives in Psychology and Christian Belief *(Baker, 1985). With her husband, Robert, she has edited* Women in Ministry: Four Views *(InterVarsity, 1989).*

Robert G. Clouse *is professor of history at Indiana State University, Terre Haute, Indiana. He is a graduate of Bryan College, Grace Theolog-*

ical Seminary, and the University of Iowa, from which he earned his doctorate. Clouse is the author of The Church in an Age of Orthodoxy and Enlightenment 1600–1800 *(Concordia, 1980). He has edited and contributed to* The Meaning of the Millennium *(InterVarsity, 1977),* War: Four Christian Views *(InterVarsity, 1981), and with his wife, Bonnidell,* Women in Ministry: Four Views *(InterVarsity, 1989). Since 1964, he has served as pastor of First Brethren Church, Clay City, Indiana.*

Wayne A. Grudem *is associate professor of biblical and systematic theology at Trinity Evangelical Divinity School, Deerfield, Illinois. He is a graduate of Harvard University, Westminster Theological Seminary, and the University of Cambridge, England, writing his doctoral dissertation on the gift of prophecy in 1 Corinthians. He is the author of* The Gift of Prophecy in the New Testament and Today *(Crossway Books, 1988), and* 1 Peter *in the Tyndale New Testament Commentary series (Eerdmans, 1988).*

Kenneth S. Kantzer *is distinguished professor of biblical and systematic theology and dean emeritus of Trinity Evangelical Divinity School, and chancellor of Trinity College, Deerfield, Illinois. A former editor of* CHRISTIANITY TODAY, *he continues to serve as a senior editor of that magazine and as dean of the Christianity Today Institute. Kantzer is a graduate of Ashland College, Ohio State University, Faith Theological Seminary, and Harvard University, from which he received his Ph.D. His publications include chapters in* Religions in a Changing World, The Evangelicals, Inspiration and Interpretation, The Word for This Century, *and* Jesus of Nazareth: Savior and Lord.

Peter Kreeft *is professor of philosophy at Boston College. He is a graduate of Calvin College and Fordham University, from which he received his M.A. and Ph.D. He is the author of 16 books and booklets, including* Heaven, The Heart's Deepest Longing *(Harper & Row, 1980). He is known for his use of the Socratic dialogue (most recently in* Socrates Meets Jesus *[InterVarsity, 1987]) and the dialogue catechism* (Prayer: The Great Conversation *[Servant, 1985]).*

David Neff *is senior associate editor of* CHRISTIANITY TODAY *and editor of the Christianity Today Institute. He is a graduate of Loma Linda University and Andrews University, and he has pursued additional graduate study at San Francisco Theological Seminary. Before coming to* CHRISTIANITY TODAY, *he served as editor of HIS, InterVarsity Christian Fellowship's erstwhile magazine for college students.*

Roger R. Nicole *is professor emeritus of theology at Gordon-Conwell Theological Seminary, South Hamilton, Massachusetts. He is a graduate of the Gymnase Classique, Lausanne, Switzerland; the Sorbonne, Paris; the Institut Biblique in Nogent/Marne, France; and Gordon Divinity School and Harvard Divinity School, from which he received the Doctor of Theology and Doctor of Philosophy degrees respectively. He is the author of* Moyse Amyrat: A Bibliography *and coauthor of* A Bibliography of B. B. Warfield.

J. I. Packer *is professor of historical and systematic theology at Regent College, Vancouver, British Columbia. He is a graduate of Oxford University, from which he received a D.Phil. His many books include* "Fundamentalism" and the Word of God *(Eerdmans, 1958),* Evangelism and the Sovereignty of God *(InterVarsity, 1961),* Knowing God *(InterVarsity, 1973), and* Keeping in Step with the Spirit *(Revell, 1984).*

Eugene H. Peterson *has served as pastor of Christ Our King Presbyterian Church in Bel Air, Maryland, since 1962. He is a graduate of Seattle Pacific University, New York Theological Seminary, and Johns Hopkins University. He is author of eleven books, including* Reversed Thunder: The Revelation of John and the Praying Imagination *(Harper and Row, 1988).*